The Jewish Book of Days

The Jewish Book of Days

WITH ILLUSTRATIONS FROM THE
COLLECTION OF THE HEBREW UNION COLLEGE
SKIRBALL MUSEUM

Hugh Lauter Levin Associates, Inc.,
NEW YORK

DISTRIBUTED BY
MACMILLAN PUBLISHING COMPANY,
NEW YORK

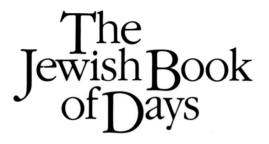

HEBREW UNION COLLEGE—JEWISH INSTITUTE OF RELIGION

The Hebrew Union College, founded in Cincinnati in 1875, is the oldest Jewish institution of higher learning in the Western hemisphere. In 1950, it merged with the Jewish Institute of Religion, established in New York in 1922. The College, long a major center of Jewish scholarship, is today a university of advanced liberal Judaic studies leading to master's and doctoral degrees. It is an international institution with four campuses: Cincinnati, New York, Los Angeles (established in 1954), and Jerusalem (developed during the early 1960s). It is also noted for its exceptional library, archival, and museum collections.

In Los Angeles, the College is developing a national institution, the Hebrew Union College Cultural Center for American Jewish Life, to expand its programs for a larger public. The Cultural Center will underscore the adventure, struggle, and opportunity America has provided its diverse religious and ethnic groups.

The College–Institute serves as an examplar in the quest to combine timeless Jewish values and modern critical methods.

Cover illustration:
Shivviti; watercolor on parchment by Solomon Attias;
North Africa, late 19th century.
Photograph H.U.C. Skirball Museum.

Frontispiece:
Torah ark miniature; silver, parcel gilt; Austria, 1783.
Photograph H.U.C. Skirball Museum.

Photography by Erich J. Hockley, John Reed Forsman, and Marvin Rand.
Designed by Robert J. O'Dell.
Edited by Stephan O. Parnes.

ISBN 0-88363-388-4
Printed in Japan

INTRODUCTION

The Jewish Book of Days is a permanent record book, not an appointment calendar. It is designed to assist you in keeping track of the important dates in your life—birthdays, wedding anniversaries, dates of death—any date that you feel is significant enough to record and to remember.

The book is arranged according to the order of the civil calendar, with a place for each day of the year. Since the dates are not associated with the days of the week, the calendar is not limited to any one year. You simply turn to the appropriate month and the appropriate day of that month to record your information. In the future, when you turn to *The Jewish Book of Days* and review the month ahead, you will be reminded of all the special dates associated with that month.

Special pages are provided to record information about family members and friends who have died: Hebrew names, dates of birth, and dates of death according to both the civil and the Jewish calendars.

Another special feature is the comparative calendar. The civil and the Jewish calendars for the years 1987 to 2000 are arranged week by week in parallel columns. This will enable you to plan meetings, vacations, and other special events without unknowingly setting up a conflict with a holiday. It will also help you to calculate the dates for Yahrzeit observances.

You and your family will always appreciate the convenience of having these records in one book. Used faithfully, *The Jewish Book of Days* will become an important family document that will be treasured many years into the future.

לתורה
וזאת התורה אשר
שם משה לפני בני
ישראל על פי ה׳ ביד
משה

JANUARY

Hank Greenberg, professional baseball player, born (1911). 1

The Jewish Theological Seminary of America opens (1887). 2

Victor Borge, pianist and comedian, born (1909). 3

Captain Alfred Dreyfus publicly degraded after wrongful conviction for espionage (1895). 4

Maryland, for the first time, allowed Jews to hold public office (1826). 5

Detail from wimpel of Gershon son of Abraham Seltz; undyed linen, polychrome pigments; Germany, 1834. Photograph H.U.C. Skirball Museum.

January

6

American Jewish Congress founded in Pittsburgh (1943).

7

Johann Philipp Reis, inventor of a telephone, born (1834).

8

Jews expelled from Genoa, Italy (1598).

9

Hayyim Nachman Bialik, Hebrew poet, born (1873).

10

Poll tax abolished in France (1784).

11

Abraham Mapu, writer believed to have written first Hebrew novel, born (1808

12

Jews expelled from Sicily (1493).

January

Emile Zola published *J'Accuse*, in defense of Captain Alfred Dreyfus (1898).

13

The Church burned confiscated Jewish books in Rome (1601).

14

Swiss Jews granted civic equality (1866).

15

Mount Sinai Hospital (New York) founded (1852).

16

Shari Lewis, puppeteer, born (1934).

17

B'nai Israel organized in Cincinnati (1824).

18

First resistance to Nazis at Warsaw Ghetto (1943).

19

January

The Federation of Jewish Farmers of America founded (1909).

20

The Women's League of the United Synagogue of America organized (1918).

21

National Federation of Temple Sisterhoods organized (1913).

22

First printing of the Pentateuch (1492).

23

First Jewish physician, Dr. Jacob Lumbrozo, settles in U.S. (1656).

24

State of Israel held the first Knesset elections (1949).

25

Auschwitz liberated by the Russian Army (1945).

26

Rimmonim (Torah finials); silver, parcel gilt, by Jeremiah Zobel; Frankfurt, Germany, early 18th century. Photograph H.U.C. Skirball Museum.

January

27

Border of Israel and Egypt opened (1980).

28

Great Britain recognized the State of Israel (1949).

29

Ezekiel Hart, the first Jew elected to the Canadian Parliament, was denied his seat because he would not be sworn in "upon the true faith of a Christian" (1808).

30

Society for Youth Aliyah established in Berlin (1933).

31

Henry II forbade Jews in England to build new synagogues (1253).

FEBRUARY

Morris J. Raphall became the first rabbi to deliver an invocation at the opening of a congressional session (1860). 1

Abba Eban, Israeli statesman, born (1915). 2

Jews reinvited to settle in the Kingdom of the Two Sicilies (1740). 3

Right of residence in England granted Luis Carvajal by Oliver Cromwell (1657). 4

Egyptian parliament voted to end the boycott of Israel (1980). 5

First auto-da-fé of the Spanish Inquisition held (1481). 6

Disputation of Tortosa opened (1413). 7

February

Louis Philippe ratified bill to place French Jews on equal terms with Catholics and Protestants (1831).

8

The French Sanhedrin opened its first session (1807).

9

British blockade of Palestine broken by ship carrying illegal immigrants (1934).

10

Jews defended the city of Worms (1201).

11

First auto-da-fé in Toledo (1486).

12

Jews of Speyer massacred (1195).

13

The Knesset opened its first session (1949).

14

eaked vase; terra-cotta, burnished; Luristan (Amlash?), ersian period. Photograph H.U.C. Skirball Museum.

February

15

The Jews of Rome removed their yellow badges (1798).

16

First new synagogue in Madrid since 149[2] dedicated (1917).

17

Chaim Weizmann elected first president of Israel (1949).

18

Israeli embassy in Cairo was opened (1980).

19

Casa dei Catecumeni (House of Convert[s]) established for converted Jews in Rome (1543).

20

The reorganized Jewish Theological Seminary of America received its new charter (1902).

21

Jews expelled from German city Ratisbo[n] (1519).

February

Land purchased for the first Jewish cemetery in New York (1656).

22

United Synagogue of America founded (1913).

23

Hadassah founded by Henrietta Szold (1912).

24

Recitation of the prayer *Aleinu* prohibited in Castile (1336).

25

The Jews were expelled from all papal territory except Rome and Ancona (1569).

26

David Sarnoff, radio pioneer, born (1891).

27

First auto-da-fé in the New World (1574).

28/29

המלך ביהודים לאבדם ואת פתשגן כתב הדת
אשר נתן בשושן להשמידם נתן לו להראות את
אסתר ולהגיד לה ולצוות עליה לבוא אל
המלך להתחנן לו ולבקש מלפניו על עמה ויבא
התך ויגד לאסתר את דברי מרדכי ותאמר
אסתר להתך ותצוהו אל מרדכי כל עבדי המלך
ועם מדינות המלך יודעים אשר כל איש ואשה
אשר יבוא אל המלך אל החצר הפנימית אשר
לא יקרא אחת דתו להמית לבד מאשר יושיט
לו המלך את שרביט הזהב וחיה ואני לא נקראתי
לבוא אל המלך זה שלושים יום ויגידו למרדכי
את דברי אסתר ויאמר מרדכי להשיב אל אסתר
אל תדמי בנפשך להמלט בית המלך מכל
היהודים כי אם החרש תחרישי בעת הזאת
רוח והצלה יעמוד ליהודים ממקום אחר ואת
ובית אביך תאבדו ומי יודע אם לעת כזאת הגעת
למלכות ותאמר אסתר להשיב אל מרדכי
לך כנוס את כל היהודים הנמצאים בשושן
וצומו עלי ואל תאכלו ואל תשתו שלשת
ימים לילה ויום גם אני ונערתי אצום כן ובכן
אבוא אל המלך אשר לא כדת וכאשר אבדתי
אבדתי ויעבר מרדכי ויעש ככל אשר צותה
עליו אסתר ויהי ביום השלישי ותלבש אסתר
מלכות ותעמד בחצר בית המלך הפנימית
נכח בית המלך והמלך יושב על כסא
מלכותו בבית המלכות נכח פתח הבית ויהי
כראות המלך את אסתר המלכה עמדת
בחצר נשאה חן בעיניו ויושט המלך לאסתר
את שרביט הזהב אשר בידו ותקרב אסתר
ותגע בראש השרביט ויאמר לה המלך מה
לך אסתר המלכה ומה בקשתך עד חצי
המלכות וינתן לך ותאמר אסתר אם על

MARCH

The Jew, the first English-language Jewish periodical in the U.S., began publication (1823).

1

Vladimir Jabotinsky formed a Jewish brigade to fight the Turks in Palestine (1915).

2

David Emanuel, first Jewish governor in the United States, sworn in (1801).

3

Religious freedom granted in Austria (1849).

4

A petition for U.S. assistance in establishing a Jewish state in Palestine, initiated by a Christian clergyman, was sent to President Harrison (1891).

5

Scroll of Esther; parchment, sepia; Venice, Italy, 1748. Photograph H.U.C. Skirball Museum.

March

6

Jerry Lewis, comedian, born (1926).

7

Rabbi Simeon ben Zemach Duran, talmudic scholar and philosopher, born (1361).

8

Cyd Charisse, dancer and actress, born (1921).

9

Pope Innocent IV ordered that the Talmud be burned (1244).

10

The Association for the Reform of Judaism was organized in Berlin (184

11

Jews of Prussia emancipated (1812).

12

Congress permits Jewish clergymen to serve as army chaplains (1862).

March

13

William Herschel, British astronomer, discovered Uranus (1781).

14

Albert Einstein, physicist, born (1879).

15

Anatoly Scharansky arrested in Moscow (1977).

16

The Pale of Settlement was abolished by the provisional government of Russia (1917).

17

Napoleon signed a decree establishing consistories, a centralized organization designed to facilitate the transformation of the Jews into French citizens (1808).

18

More than eighty French Jews were burned at the stake in a massacre at Bray (1191).

19

Philip Roth, writer, born (1933).

ונתון הלבוש והסוס
על יד איש משרי המלך
הפרתמים והלבשו את האיש אשר
המלך חפץ ביקרו והרכיבהו על הסוס
ברחוב העיר וקראו לפניו ככה יעשה לאיש
אשר המלך חפץ ביקרו ויאמר המלך להמן
מהר קח את הלבוש ואת הסוס כאשר דברת ועשה כן
למרדכי היהודי הישב בשער המלך אל תפל דבר מכל
אשר דברת ויקח המן את הלבוש ואת הסוס וילבש
את מרדכי וירכיבהו ברחוב העיר ויקרא לפניו ככה
יעשה לאיש אשר המלך חפץ ביקרו וישב מרדכי אל
שער המלך והמן נדחף אל ביתו אבל וחפוי ראש ויספר
המן לזרש אשתו ולכל אהביו את כל אשר קרהו ויאמרו
לו חכמיו וזרש אשתו אם מזרע היהודים מרדכי אשר
החלות לנפל לפניו לא תוכל לו כי נפול תפול לפניו
עודם מדברים עמו וסריסי המלך הגיעו ויבהלו
להביא את המן אל המשתה אשר עשתה אסתר
ויבא המלך והמן לשתות עם אסתר המלכה ויאמר
המלך לאסתר גם ביום השני במשתה היין מה שאלתך
אסתר המלכה ותנתן לך ומה בקשתך עד חצי המלכות

Rabbi Isaac Elchanan Theological Seminary founded (1897).

20

Spain granted legal status to the Jewish community (1965).

21

The first YMHA was established in New York (1874).

22

The Zion Mule Corps, a Jewish auxiliary unit of the British Army, was formed (1915).

23

Printing of Talmud permitted in Italy (1564).

24

Shaaare Chesed (later called the Touro Synagogue), the first congregation in New Orleans, was incorporated (1828).

25

Peace treaty between Egypt and Israel signed (1979).

26

Scroll of Esther; parchment, ink and tempera; Germany, about 1700. Photograph H.U.C. Skirball Museum.

March

27

Po'ale Zion in the United States began to publish *Der Yidisher Kemfer* (1906).

28

Turkish authorities expelled Jews from Jaffa and Tel Aviv (1917).

29

Jews of Sardinia emancipated (1848).

30

Papal Bull prohibited Jewish physicians from treating Christian patients (1581).

31

King Ferdinand and Queen Isabella signed the order expelling Jews from Spain (1492).

APRIL

Hebrew University of Jerusalem formally opened by Lord Balfour (1925). 1

Over 100,000 Jews expelled from Sicily (1492). 2

Israel and Jordan signed an armistice agreement (1949). 3

Jews granted complete equality by the Russian government (1917). 4

The Polish army executed thirty-five Jews for handing out Joint Distribution Committee packages to the Jews of Pinsk (1919). 5

April

Jews of Prussia emancipated (1848). **6**

Michael Cardoso received the right to practice law in Brazil from the Dutch West India Co. (1645). **7**

Congregation Shearith Israel (New York) dedicated the first synagogue building built in North America (1730). **8**

The Jewish Welfare Board was founded (1917). **9**

The Falashas were recognized as Jews by the State of Israel (1975). **10**

City of Tel Aviv founded (1909). **11**

The Knesset passed a resolution designating Nisan 27 as Yom ha-Shoah (1951). **12**

Detail of Rondels Haggadah; parchment, ink and tempera; Italy, first half of 15th century. Photograph H.U.C. Skirball Museum.

April

13

Sabato Morais, first president of the Jewish Theological Seminary of America, born (1823).

14

Rod Steiger, actor, born (1925).

15

Rabbi Stephen S. Wise founded the Free Synagogue in New York (1907).

16

Jews in the German Empire emancipated (1871).

17

The gates of the ghetto of Rome were pulled down by the citizens of Rome (1848).

18

Maimonides departed North Africa for Palestine (1165).

19

The Warsaw Ghetto revolt began (1943).

April

20

The Supreme Council of the Peace Conference at San Remo recognized the Balfour Declaration and made Palestine a British Mandate (1920).

21

Shehitah prohibited in Germany (1933).

22

Adolphe Crémieux, founder of Alliance Israelite Universelle, born (1796).

23

Jews prohibited from remaining in France (1615).

24

Barbara Streisand, singer and actress, born (1942).

25

The Israel-Egypt peace treaty took effect (1979).

26

Jews permitted to settle in New Amsterdam (1655).

חג המצות
מבית חנוך ילדים
בעהק ירושלם תו

April

Anouk Aimée, actress, born (1932).

27

A pogrom at Elizavetgrad was followed by a series of pogroms throughout the Ukraine and neighboring provinces (1881).

28

Elliot Gould, actor, born (1938).

29

A royal proclamation instructs Jews to leave Spain by the end of July (1492).

30

atzah cover; velvet, silk and metallic embroidery, shells, quins, papier-mâché; the Orphan's School, Jerusalem, early 0th century. Photograph H.U.C. Skirball Museum.

MAY

1

Mizrachi Organization of America founded (1914).

2

Theodor Herzl, founder of the World Zionist Organization, born (1860).

3

The YMHA constitution was adopted (1874).

4

Roberta Peters, opera singer, born (1930).

5

Karl Marx, political philosopher, born (1818).

May

Sigmund Freud, founder of psychoanalysis, born (1856).

6

Empress Catherine I ordered all Jews expelled from the Ukraine (1727).

7

The first printed set of Mishnah with the commentary of Maimonides was published in Naples (1492).

8

Mike Wallace, TV interviewer, born (1918).

9

A provincial Church Council meeting in Vienna reaffirmed anti-Jewish legislation of the Fourth Lateran Council (1267).

10

Israel admitted to UN (1949).

11

First class graduated from Hebrew University–Hadassah Medical School (1952).

12

May

Nonnative Jews expelled from Bohemia (1763).

13

U.S. recognized the State of Israel (1948).

14

Warsaw Ghetto uprising ended (1943).

15

Al Jolson, singer, born (1886).

16

Soviet Union recognized the State of Israel (1948).

17

Czechoslovakia, Nicaragua, Poland, and Uruguay recognized the State of Israel (1948).

18

Iraqi Jews began to depart for Israel (1950).

19

mer calendar; silver, coral, ink and tempera on archment, by Maurice Meyer; France, mid-19th century. hotograph H.U.C. Skirball Museum.

May

20

Emil Berliner, American who invented gramophone, born (1851).

21

John Garfield, actor, born (1912).

22

Native-born Jews granted citizenship by Romania (1919).

23

Artie Shaw, band leader, born (1910).

24

Bob Dylan, folk singer, born (1941).

25

Beverly Sills, opera singer, born (1929

26

Fifty-one French Jews were killed in a massacre at Blois (1171).

27

Portuguese Inquisition suspended by Pope Innocent XI (1679).

28

By order of Pope Clement XII, all Hebrew books in the Papal States were confiscated (1731).

29

Jews of the Ottoman Empire granted equal rights (1453).

30

Napoleon called for assembly of Jewish leaders (1806).

31

Sigismund III of Poland unsuccessfully tried to keep Jews out of Riga and the province of Livonia (1593).

JUNE

Israel and the Arab states agreed to a cease-fire (1948). 1

Emanuel Bessels, explorer of the North Pole, born (1847). 2

The Jewish Publication Society of America was founded (1888). 3

Beth Hamedrash became the first congregation organized by Russian Jews in the U.S. (1852). 4

Canadian Jews received equal rights (1832). 5

Ketubbah; parchment, tempera and ink; Busseto, Italy, 1677. Frame; second half of 18th century. Photograph H.U.C. Skirball Museum.

June

6

I. M. Rabbinowitz, rabbinical author and physician, born (1818).

7

Jerusalem was reunited (1967).

8

The Union of Orthodox Jewish Congregations of America was founded (1898).

9

The Synagogue Council of America wa founded (1925).

10

Isaac Miranda, first Jewish judge in America, appointed (1727).

11

Ha-Ẓofeh ba-Areẓ ha-Ḥadashah, the fir Hebrew periodical in the U.S., began publication (1871).

12

Talmud placed on trial at Disputation Paris (1240).

June

13

Paulette Goddard, actress, born (1911).

14

Directors of West India Company ordered Peter Stuyvesant to allow Jews to trade at New Amsterdam's different outposts (1656).

15

Many Jews were killed in a riot in Safed (1834).

16

Jews expelled from Florence (1527).

17

Talmud burned in Paris (1242).

18

Jemal Pasha prohibited Jews from praying at the Wailing (Western) Wall because their prayers include a plea for the reestablishment of a Jewish State (1915).

19

Louis IX of France decreed all Jews must wear yellow badge (1269).

ולחופה

June

20 Samson Rafael Hirsch, founder of modern Orthodoxy, born (1808).

21 Jacques Offenbach, composer, born (1819).

22 Jewish section of Prague destroyed by fire (1689).

23 Six-year-old Edgardo Mortara, of Bologna, abducted by papal police to be raised as Roman Catholic (1858).

24 The Russian Ministry of the Interior instructed local authorities to suppress Zionism among the Jews (1903).

25 The kibbutz Rishon le-Zion was founded (1882).

26 Peter Lorre, actor, born (1904).

Detail of wimpel; undyed linen, polychrome pigment; Germany, 1777. Photograph H.U.C. Skirball Museum.

June

27

The Yiddish newspaper *Die Yidishe Velt* began publication in New York (1902).

28

Old City of Jerusalem united with the New City (1967).

29

The Lovers of Zion, an American Zionist organization, was organized (1897).

30

Auto-da-fé held in Madrid to honor marriage of Carlos II and Louise Marie d'Orléans (1680).

JULY

omanian Jews granted political equality
1879). 1

nglo-Jewish Association founded (1871). 2

he first complete edition of Jacob ben
sher's code, the *Arba'ah Turim*,
ublished (1475). 3

n Landers and Abigail van Buren,
dvice columnists, born (1918). 4

aron David Günzberg, Jewish scholar,
orn (1857). 5

July

6 First members of Bilu, an early Zionist organization, arrive in Jaffa from Russia (1882).

7 Secular education required for Galician rabbis (1836).

8 Jacob Barsimson, first Jew to arrive in New Amsterdam, set sail (1654).

9 First Lord Rothschild to take seat in House of Commons (1885).

10 Camille Pisarro, painter, born (1830).

11 Jews expelled from Little Russia (1739).

12 Milton Berle, comedian, born (1908).

orah crown; silver, parcel gilt; Eastern Europe, 9th century. Photograph H.U.C. Skirball Museum.

July

13

Jerusalem captured by Crusaders (1096).

14

Isaac Bashevis Singer, Nobel Prize-winning novelist, born (1904).

15

Spanish Inquisition abolished (1834).

16

Graziadio Isaiah Ascoli, founder of philology in Italy, born (1829).

17

Israel Jacobson opened first Reform synagogue, in Seesen, Westphalia (1810)

18

British seize *The Exodus, 1947*, carrying 4,000 people (1947).

19

Thirty-eight Jews burned in Brandenbu as a result of a Host-desecration libel (1810).

July

20

Disputation of Barcelona opened (1263).

21

Harbor of Haifa opened (1933).

22

ews of France arrested at order of King
Philip IV (1306).

23

habbetai Zvi, false messiah, born (1626).

24

ynagogues of Posen sacked and Torahs
esecrated (1716).

25

nperor Leopold I expelled the Jews
om Vienna (1670).

26

quisition established in Rome (1267).

July

Benedict Spinoza excommunicated (1656).

27

Clement Freud, grandson of Sigmund Freud, elected to Knesset (1974).

28

The Union of Orthodox Rabbis of the United States and Canada was founded (1902).

29

Citizens of Nuremburg forbidden to borrow from Jews (1539).

30

Nachman Krochmal, Jewish philosopher, born (1840).

31

abbath Afternoon ***(detail); oil on canvas by Moritz Oppenheim; ermany, 19th century. Photograph H.U.C. Skirball Museum.***

AUGUST

1

Di Post, the first Yiddish periodical in the United States, began publication (1870).

2

Jews leave Spain (1492).

3

The Twentieth World Zionist Congress was held (1937).

4

Pope Nicholas III required Jews to attend sermons intended to convert them (1278).

5

More than three hundred Jews were killed in a massacre in Barcelona (1391).

August

Marcus Eliezer Bloch, ichthyologist, born (1799). 6

Bar-Ilan University was founded (1955). 7

Jacob Christian Basnage, author of first modern history of Jews, born (1653). 8

The Tenth World Zionist Congress, the first to conduct its meetings in Hebrew, met in Basle (1911). 9

Zacharias Frankel became the president of the Jewish Theological Seminary of Breslau, a new rabbinical school that he had helped establish (1854). 10

Marranos who escaped from Spain fall victim to auto-da-fé in Lima (1635). 11

"Death of the Poets" ordered by Stalin kills 24 Yiddish writers (1952). 12

August

Joan Blondell, actress, born (1909). 13

Felix Adler, founder of Ethical Culture Society, born (1851). 14

The Third Zionist Congress met in Basle (1899). 15

Laws regulating the condition of the Jews of Saxony issued (1838). 16

Larry Rivers, painter, born (1923). 17

Jew's Oath abolished in Austria (1846). 18

Maximillian I orders the destruction of Jewish books (1509). 19

Torah case; silver, coral and semiprecious stones; Nablus, Land of Israel, 1756. Photograph H.U.C. Skirball Museum.

August

20

Shehitah prohibited in Switzerland (1893).

21

The English Parliament passed the Sheriff's Declaration Bill, allowing Jews to serve as sheriffs (1835).

22

Jacob Barsimson landed in New Amsterdam, becoming the first known Jew to settle in North America (1654).

23

Jews throughout Palestine were attacked, and many were killed, by Arab rioters (1929).

24

Operation Magic Carpet was officially concluded after bringing 45,000 Yemenite Jews to Israel (1950).

25

British allowed illegal Jewish immigrants who had been held on Mauritius to enter Palestine (1945).

26

The infamous forgery *The Protocols of the Elders of Zion* was published (serially) for the first time (1903).

August

27

Tzar Nicholas II approved Cabinet decision to grant Jews right of residence in cities and towns beyond the Pale of Settlement except for Petrograd and Moscow (1915).

28

The Baron de Hirsch Fund founded a Jewish Agricultural colony at Woodbine, New Jersey (1891).

29

The first World Zionist Congress opened in Basle (1897).

30

The Fifteenth World Zionist Congress met in Basle (1927).

31

Itzhak Perlman, violinist, born (1945).

SEPTEMBER

The Twelfth World Zionist Congress met in Carlsbad, Czechoslovakia (1921). **1**

The Jews of Holland were emancipated (1796). **2**

Many Jews were killed in a riot that broke out during the coronation of Richard the Lion-Hearted (1189). **3**

The Arbeiter Ring (The Workman's Circle) was founded (1900). **4**

The Jews of Bologna were emancipated (1796). **5**

Shofar; Germany, mid-19th century. Case; mahogany, by Marcus Jonas; United States, late 19th century. Photograph H.U.C. Skirball Museum.

September

6

Israel participated in the First International Moscow Book Fair (1977).

7

Twenty-three Jews from Recife, Brazil, landed in New Amsterdam (1654).

8

The foundation stone of the first synagogue building in North America wa laid by Congregation Shearith Israel of New York (1729).

9

The first synagogue built in modern times in Basle, Switzerland, was dedicated (1867).

10

The Jewish community in Berlin was established (1671).

11

Jewish Colonial Association founded by Baron Maurice de Hirsch (1881).

12

The first Jewish congregational prayer service held in Manhattan (1654).

September

13
'he first synagogue in Amsterdam, Beth acob, was dedicated (1597).

14
'he Supreme Court of Israel was naugurated (1948).

15
Iordecai Manuel Noah founded Ararat, n unsuccessful Jewish colony in New ork State (1825).

16
auren Bacall, actress, born (1924).

17
ws expelled from France by King harles VI (1394).

18
reat Synagogue opened in London 772).

19
ne German government forbade the nployment of non-Jewish women in wish homes and businesses (1940).

September

Arnold "Red" Auerbach, basketball coach, born (1917).

20

Swedish government revoked privileges previously granted Swedish Jews (1838).

21

Henry Kissinger became the first Jew to serve as Secretary of State of the United States (1973).

22

New York's General Assembly resolved that Jews should not vote for representatives (1737).

23

King Louis XIV ordered Jews expelled from French possessions in America (1683).

24

Barbara Walters, television interviewer, born (1931).

25

George Gershwin, composer, born (1898).

26

Yom Kippur belt buckle; silver; Eastern Europe, early 20th century. Photograph H.U.C. Skirball Museum.

September

27

Jews of France emancipated (1791).

28

First Jewish congregation in Stockholm founded (1775).

29

Hassidim excommunicated in Cracow (1785).

30

The Portuguese Synagogue in London was dedicated (1701).

OCTOBER

'he Jewish Institute of Religion nondenominational rabbinical seminary) ›pened (1922). 1

irst public Jewish prayer services held in ımsterdam (1596). 2

Iebrew Union College opened (1875). 3

·ws deprived of rights by the Vichy overnment in France (1940). 4

ıdwig IX expelled the Jews from Lower ıvaria (1450). 5

October

The Yom Kippur War began (1973).

6

The first session of the Asefat ha-Nivḥarim (Elected Assembly), the supreme governing body of the Jewish community in Palestine, was held (1920).

7

Ohole Shem Association founded in New York to promote and foster the study of Hebrew and of Jewish history and literature (1895).

8

Czar Alexander I appointed commission to consider how to improve the condition of Russian Jews (1802).

9

Rodeph Sholom, a German-Jewish organization, was founded in Philadelphia (1802).

10

Ha-Meliẓ, the first Hebrew newspaper in Russia, began publication in Odessa as a weekly (1860).

11

Maimonides arrived in Jerusalem (1165).

12

Sukkot in Jerusalem *(detail); hand-colored etching; Augsburg, Germany, 18th century. Photograph H.U.C. Skirball Museum.*

October

13

Italy granted Jews equality and abolished the Rome ghetto (1870).

14

Foundation stone of the Knesset building was laid in Jerusalem (1958).

15

Captain Alfred Dreyfus was arrested and charged with espionage against France (1894).

16

David Ben-Gurion, Israeli statesman, bor (1886).

17

Tzar Paul I ordered censorship of Jewis books in Russia (1796).

18

The Nuremberg War Crime Trials bega (1945).

19

The Jewish Spectator, the first Jewish weekly in the southern U.S., founded i Memphis (1885).

October

British White Paper on Palestine issued (1930).

20

Emperor Joseph II of Austria abolished distinctive Jewish dress (1781).

21

UN calls for cease-fire to end Yom Kippur War (1973).

22

Jews in Barbados forbidden to engage in retail trade (1668).

23

Jews of Algeria were emancipated (1870).

24

Maimonides College opened in Philadelphia (1867).

25

Poland passed anti-Kashrut laws (1939).

26

October

27

Last public auto-da-fè held in Portugal (1765).

28

Sir Moses Montefiore, English philanthropist and social leader, born (1784).

29

All the Jews of Hesse-Cassel except peddlers and petty traders were granted full equality (1833).

30

Pope Innocent XI forbade Jews in Rome to engage in banking (1682).

31

Date by which Jews had to leave Portugal (1497).

Tallit, tallit bag, tefillin bag; silk with silk embroidery; China, 1904. Photograph H.U.C. Skirball Museum.

NOVEMBER

1

Hadoar, the first Hebrew daily newspaper began publication (1921).

2

Balfour Declaration issued (1917).

3

Jews expelled from France and French domains (1394).

4

Israeli army captured strategic Egyptian military position at Ras Natsrani (1956).

5

One of the earliest synagogues in the New World, Beracha Ve Salom of Surinam, was dedicated (1685).

November

The first international Zionist convention was held in Kattowitz, Poland (1884).

6

Leon Trotsky, Russian statesman, born (1879).

7

Operation "Magic Carpet," which brought Jews from Yemen to Israel, began (1949).

8

Kristallnacht (1938).

9

Jew's College, a rabbinical seminary, opened in London (1856).

10

Israel and Egypt signed a cease-fire agreement (1973).

11

The first B'nai B'rith lodge was organized in New York (1843).

12

November

13 The bishop of Kamenets-Podolski burned all the copies of the Talmud in his diocese after first forcing the Jews to take part in a disputation with the Frankists (1757).

14 Leopold Hilsner found guilty (later pardoned) in Blood Libel trial in Bohemia (1900).

15 Jews were no longer permitted to attend German schools (1938).

16 Yeshiva College became the first American university under Jewish auspices (1945).

17 Italy instituted its own version of the anti-Semitic Nuremberg Laws earlier put into effect by Germany (1938).

18 The first printed edition of *Ḥovot ha-Levavot*, by Baḥya ibn Paquda, was published in Naples (1489).

19 Egyptian President Anwar Sadat arrived in Israel (1977).

Torah case; wood, red lacquer, gilt, bronze hinges; Kaifeng, China, 17th century. Photograph H.U.C. Skirball Museum.

November

20

Father Coughlin delivers his first anti-Semitic attack over the radio (1938).

21

Goldie Hawn, actress, born (1945).

22

The Anti-Nazi League was incorporated (1933).

23

The Jews were expelled from Naples (1510).

24

Ha-Arukh, a dictionary of the Talmud by Rabbi Nathan ben Yehiel of Rome, was completed (1105).

25

The first American Jewish civic and soci[al] club was founded in Newport, R.I. (1761

26

The Council of Clermont proclaimed the First Crusade, an undertaking that led to the massacre of many Jewish communities, especially in the Rhine Valley (1095).

November

27

Chaim Weizmann, first president of Israel, born (1874).

28

Hans Frank, the German governor-general of the occupied territories of Poland, decreed that Jewish Councils be established (1939).

29

UN General Assembly adopted a resolution requiring the establishment of a Jewish state in Palestine (1947).

30

Congregation Mikveh Israel of Savannah, Georgia, was chartered (1790).

ויקח שמואל

DECEMBER

Voody Allen, actor, writer, and producer, born (1935). 1

Touro Synagogue in Newport, R.I., dedicated (1763). 2

harles II of Sweden barred Jews from ettling in Stockholm (1685). 3

he Whitehall Conference, discussing the eadmission of Jews to England, opened 1655). 4

ws were ordered to leave Portugal .496). 5

anukkah menorah; silver, parcel gilt; Germany, 1814. hotograph H.U.C. Skirball Museum.

December

6

The first Yiddish newspaper, the *Direnfurter Privilegirte Zeitung*, was published in Germany (1771).

7

Eli Wallach, actor, born (1915).

8

Luis de Carvajal "the Younger," writer and nephew of the governor of the Spanish territory of the New Kingdoms c Leon, was burned at the stake by the Inquisition in Mexico City (1596).

9

Kirk Douglas, actor, born (1920).

10

Nelly Sachs, poet and winner of Nobel Prize for literature, born (1891).

11

Emperor Constantine the Great made th first documented mention of Jew in Germany (321).

12

Edward G. Robinson, actor, born (1893

December

The Knesset voted to transfer Israel's capital to Jerusalem (1949).

13

Board of Deputies of British Jews established (1760).

14

The first meeting of the American Jewish Congress was held (1918).

15

Jews were expelled from France (1394).

16

General Ulysses S. Grant issued "Order No. 11," expelling all Jews from the Department of Tennessee (1862).

17

ews expelled from Prague, Bohemia, and Moravia (1774).

18

ongregation Beth Elohim, the fourth oldest synagogue in the U.S., was dedicated (1794).

19

December

Canada recognized the State of Israel (1948).

20

The Jews of Austria were emancipated (1867).

21

The department of Jewish Studies at the Hebrew University of Jerusalem was dedicated (1924).

22

The Jews of Hungary were emancipated 1867).

23

Jew York Morning Journal reported that ight members of the British cabinet ivor establishment of a strong Jewish ettlement in Palestine after the war 1915).

24

ing Frederick III of Sicily required all ws to wear a badge (1369).

25

he Israel Philharmonic Orchestra was unded (1936).

26

anukkah menorah; silver, filigree, parcel gilt; Eastern rope, mid-19th century. Photograph H.U.C. Skirball Museum.

December

27

Jews were prohibited from practicing medicine in Romania (1868).

28

The organizational meeting of the National Council of Young Israel was held (1912).

29

The Jewish National Fund was established (1901).

30

Sandy Koufax, baseball player, born (1935).

31

Empress Catherine of Russia restricted the area in which Jews were allowed reside, beginning the Pale of Settleme (1791).

THE CALENDAR

The calendar on the following pages is designed to enable you to convert dates from the civil calendar to the Jewish calendar and from the Jewish calendar to the civil calendar for civil calendar years 1987–2000. You will be able to use this calendar to help you in your planning needs. For example, since the Yahrzeit is observed on the date of death according to the Jewish calendar, all you need to do is to locate the appropriate date on the Jewish calendar and find the corresponding date on the civil calendar to the left. If you do not know the date according to the Jewish calendar, all you need to do is to locate the appropriate date on the civil calendar and check the corresponding date on the Jewish calendar to the right. (If, however, the death occurred in a year earlier than 1987, you will have to check the civil calendar date in one of several published comparative calendars in order to determine the equivalent date on the Jewish calendar.)

בסימנא טבא ובמזלא מעליא

ויתן להם מקום בראש הקרואים והמה כשלשים איש

ויעש המלך משתה גדול לכל שריו ועבדיו את משתה אסתר

מצא

אשה מצא טוב

בששי בשבת שלשה ימים להדש אלול שנת חמשת אלפים וחמש מאות וששים ושמנה לבריאת עולם למנין שאנו מנין פה ספיניאה [illegible] הרהתן הנעים יקר ונעלה כמר שמואל ניסים יצו בר המנוח כ' שמואל ברוך פנצי זל אמר לה להדא בתולתא צניעתא מרת אסתר מבת בת הנכבד יקר ונעלה כמר רפאל יאקור יצו הוי לי לאנתו כדת משה וישראל ואנא בסייעתא דשמיא אפלה ואוקיר ואזון ואפרנס ואכלכל ואכסי יתיכי כהלכת גברין יהודאין דפלחין ומוקרין וזנין ומפרנסין ית נשיהון בקושטא. ויהיבנא ליכי מהר בתוליכי כסף זוזי מאתן דחזו ליכי ומזונכי וכסותיכי וספוקיכי ומיעל לותיכי כארח כל ארעא. וצביאת מרת אסתר כלתא בתולתא דא והות ליה לאנתו. ודא נדונא דהנעלת ליה מבי אבוה יצו הנל דוקאטי חמשת אלפים לערך שש ליטרין וד' סולדי הדוקאטו מהולקים בזה האופן דוקאטי שלשת אלפים לערך הנל בכל כך מעות מחושבים. ודוקאטי שני אלפים לערך הנל בכל כך מטלטלים ובגדים של משי צמר ופשתים ועדיי זהב וכסף השייכים לגוף הכלה הנל. וצבי ההתן יצו הנל והוסיף לה ממעונה על הנדוניא הנל בתורת תוספת ומאתן זוזי להראות כמה חבתו לכלתו הנל סך אלף ושש מאות וששים ושש דוקאטי ושני ליטרין ושלשה עשר סולדי דהיינו השליש מכל הנדוניא הנל בקירוב. הכל כאשר לכל כפי שנתבאר בשטר השידוכין מלבד טבעת הקידושין. וכך אמר לנא ההתן הנעים יצו הנל אחריות כתובתא דא נדוניא ותוספתא כנל קבלית עלי ועל ירתי בתראי להתפרעא מן כל שפר ארג נכסין וקנינן דאית לי תחות כל שמיא דקנאי ודאקני נכסין דאית להון אחריות ודלית להון אחריות כלהון יהון אחראין וערבאין עלי למגבא מנהון נדוניא ותוספתא אילין עד גמירא ואפילו מן גלימא דעל כתפאי בחיי ובמותא מן יומא דנן ולעלם. וקבל עליו ההתן יצו הנל חומר וחיזוק שטרא דא כאחריות וחומר כל שטרי כתובות דנהיגי בישראל העשויין כהוגן וכתיקון חזל הכל דלא כאסמכתא ודלא כטופסי דשטרי בביטול כל מיני מודעי ותולדותיהן עד סופן ובפיסול עידיהן פיסול תורה לדעת הרשבא זל. וקנינא אנן סהדי דהתימי לתתא מיד ההתן הנעים כ' שמואל ניסים יצו הנל לזכות הכלה המהוללה מרת אסתר מבת הנל ולזכות יורשיה ובאי כחה קנין גמור ושלם במנא דכשר למקניא ביה מעכשו על כל מאי דכתיב ומפרש לעיל וביום ד' כר אנוסטו אלף ותתח למנינם החתן וכלתו הלכו לפני האופיציאל ציויל ואמרו שרוצים להזדווג זעז והאופיציאל הכריז כפני העומדים שנעשה הזיווג כפי חקי הקודיצי ציויל ועם מלות ספיניאה עד בארת דעל הנרר ודין קיומייהו דהכל שריר ובריר וקים

ויגדל שמואל וה' היה עמו

אשריך וטוב לך: אשתך כגפן פוריה בירכתי ביתך בניך כשתילי זיתים ומ'

שיר המעלות אשרי כל ירא ה' ההולך בדרכיו: יגיע כפיך כי תאכל אשריך

'87 CIVIL CALENDAR JEWISH CALENDAR 5747

	S	M	T	W	T	F	S	S	M	T	W	T	F	S		
JAN					1	2	3					**30** Ḥanukkah	**1** Ḥanukkah	**2** Ḥanukkah	Mi-Keẓ	KIS/TEV
	4	5	6	7	8	9	10	3	4	5	6	7	8	9	Va-Yiggash	
	11	12	13	14	15	16	17	**10** Fast of Tevet	11	12	13	14	15	16	Va-Yeḥi	
	18	19	20	21	22	23	24	17	18	19	20	21	22	23	Shemot	
	25	26	27	28	29	30	31	24	25	26	27	28	29	**1**	Va-Era	SHEV
EB	1	2	3	4	5	6	7	2	3	4	5	6	7	8	Bo	
	8	9	10	11	12	13	14	9	10	11	12	13	14	**15** Tu bi-Shevat	Be-Shallaḥ Shabbat Shirah	
	15	16	17	18	19	20	21	16	17	18	19	20	21	22	Yitro	
	22	23	24	25	26	27	28	23	24	25	26	27	28	29	Mishpatim Shabbat Shekalim	
AR	1	2	3	4	5	6	7	**30**	**1**	2	3	4	5	6	Terumah	ADAR
	8	9	10	11	12	13	14	7	8	9	10	**11** Fast of Esther	12	13	Teẓavveh Shabbat Zakhor	
	15	16	17	18	19	20	21	**14** Purim	**15** Shushan Purim	16	17	18	19	20	Ki Tissa Shabbat Parah	
	22	23	24	25	26	27	28	21	22	23	24	25	26	27	Va-Yakhel/Pekudei Shabbat ha-Ḥodesh	
PR	29	30	31	1	2	3	4	28	29	**1**	2	3	4	5	Va-Yikra	NIS
	5	6	7	8	9	10	11	6	7	8	9	10	11	12	Ẓav Shabbat ha-Gadol	
	12	13	14	15	16	17	18	13	14	**15** Pesaḥ	**16** Pesaḥ	**17** Ḥol ha-Mo'ed	**18** Ḥol ha-Mo'ed	**19** Ḥol ha-Mo'ed	Ḥol ha-Mo'ed	
	19	20	21	22	23	24	25	**20** Ḥol ha-Mo'ed	**21** Pesaḥ	**22** Pesaḥ	23	24	25	26	Shemini	
AY	26	27	28	29	30	1	2	**27** Yom ha-Sho'ah	28	29	**30**	**1**	2	3	Tazri'a/Meẓora	IYAR
	3	4	5	6	7	8	9	4	**5** Yom ha-Aẓma'ut	6	7	8	9	10	Aḥarei Mot/ Kedoshim	
	10	11	12	13	14	15	16	11	12	13	14	15	16	17	Emor	
	17	18	19	20	21	22	23	**18** Lag ba-Omer	19	20	21	22	23	24	Be-Har/Ḥukkotai	
	24	25	26	27	28	29	30	25	26	27	**28** Yom Yerushalayim	29	**1**	2	Be-Midbar	SIV
NE	31	1	2	3	4	5	6	3	4	5	**6** Shavuot	**7** Shavuot	8	9	Naso	
	7	8	9	10	11	12	13	10	11	12	13	14	15	16	Be-Ha'alotkha	
	14	15	16	17	18	19	20	17	18	19	20	21	22	23	Shelaḥ	
	21	22	23	24	25	26	27	24	25	26	27	28	29	**30**	Koraḥ	
	28	29	30					**1**	2	3						TAM

tubbah; parchment, tempera and ink; Spinea,
ly, 1808. Photograph H.U.C. Skirball Museum.

1987 CIVIL CALENDAR — JEWISH CALENDAR 5747/48

	S	M	T	W	T	F	S	S	M	T	W	T	F	S		
JULY				1	2	3	4				4	5	6	7	Ḥukkat	TAM
	5	6	7	8	9	10	11	8	9	10	11	12	13	14	Balak	
	12	13	14	15	16	17	18	15	16	**17** Fast of Tammuz	18	19	20	21	Pinḥas	
	19	20	21	22	23	24	25	22	23	24	25	26	27	28	Mattot/Masei	
	26	27	28	29	30	31	1	29	**1**	2	3	4	5	6	Devarim Shabbat Ḥazon	AV
AUG	2	3	4	5	6	7	8	7	8	**9** Fast of Av	10	11	12	13	Va-Etḥannan Shabbat Naḥamu	
	9	10	11	12	13	14	15	14	15	16	17	18	19	20	Ekev	
	16	17	18	19	20	21	22	21	22	23	24	25	26	27	Re'eh	
	23	24	25	26	27	28	29	28	29	**30**	**1**	2	3	4	Shofetim	ELUL
SEP	30	31	1	2	3	4	5	5	6	7	8	9	10	11	Ki Teẓe	
	6	7	8	9	10	11	12	12	13	14	15	16	17	18	Ki Tavo	
	13	14	15	16	17	18	19	19	20	21	22	23	24	25	Niẓẓavim/Va-Yelekh	
	20	21	22	23	24	25	26	26	27	28	29	**1** Rosh ha-Shanah	**2** Rosh ha-Shanah	3	Ha'azinu Shabbat Shuvah	5748
OCT	27	28	29	30	1	2	3	**4** Fast of Gedaliah	5	6	7	8	9	**10** Yom Kippur	Yom Kippur	TISH
	4	5	6	7	8	9	10	11	12	13	14	**15** Sukkot	**16** Sukkot	**17** Ḥol ha-Mo'ed	Ḥol ha-Mo'ed	
	11	12	13	14	15	16	17	**18** Ḥol ha-Mo'ed	**19** Ḥol ha-Mo'ed	**20** Ḥol ha-Mo'ed	**21** Hoshana Rabba	**22** Shemini Aẓeret	**23** Simḥat Torah	24	Bereshit	
	18	19	20	21	22	23	24	25	26	27	28	29	**30**	**1**	No'aḥ	ḤESH
	25	26	27	28	29	30	31	2	3	4	5	6	7	8	Lekh Lekha	
NOV	1	2	3	4	5	6	7	9	10	11	12	13	14	15	Va-Yera	
	8	9	10	11	12	13	14	16	17	18	19	20	21	22	Ḥayyei Sarah	
	15	16	17	18	19	20	21	23	24	25	26	27	28	29	Toledot	
	22	23	24	25	26	27	28	**1**	2	3	4	5	6	7	Va-Yeẓe	KIS
DEC	29	30	1	2	3	4	5	8	9	10	11	12	13	14	Va-Yishlaḥ	
	6	7	8	9	10	11	12	15	16	17	18	19	20	21	Va-Yeshev	
	13	14	15	16	17	18	19	22	23	24	**25** Ḥanukkah	**26** Ḥanukkah	**27** Ḥanukkah	**28** Ḥanukkah	Mi-Keẓ	
	20	21	22	23	24	25	26	**29** Ḥanukkah	**30** Ḥanukkah	**1** Ḥanukkah	**2** Ḥanukkah	3	4	5	Va-Yiggash	
	27	28	29	30	31			6	7	8	9	**10** Fast of Tevet				TEV

	CIVIL CALENDAR 1988							JEWISH CALENDAR 5748								
	S	M	T	W	T	F	S	S	M	T	W	T	F	S		
JAN						1	2						11	12	Va-Yeḥi	TEV
	3	4	5	6	7	8	9	13	14	15	16	17	18	19	Shemot	
	10	11	12	13	14	15	16	20	21	22	23	24	25	26	Va-Era	
	17	18	19	20	21	22	23	27	28	29	**1**	2	3	4	Bo	SHEV
	24	25	26	27	28	29	30	5	6	7	8	9	10	11	Be-Shallaḥ Shabbat Shirah	
FEB	31	1	2	3	4	5	6	12	13	14	**15** Tu bi-Shevat	16	17	18	Yitro	
	7	8	9	10	11	12	13	19	20	21	22	23	24	25	Mishpatim Shabbat Shekalim	
	14	15	16	17	18	19	20	26	27	28	29	**30**	**1**	2	Terumah	ADAR
	21	22	23	24	25	26	27	3	4	5	6	7	8	9	Teẓavveh Shabbat Zakhor	
MAR	28	29	1	2	3	4	5	10	11	12	**13** Fast of Esther	**14** Purim	**15** Shushan Purim	16	Ki Tissa	
	6	7	8	9	10	11	12	17	18	19	20	21	22	23	Va-Yakhel/Pekudei Shabbat Parah	
	13	14	15	16	17	18	19	24	25	26	27	28	29	**1**	Va-Yikra Shabbat ha-Ḥodesh	NIS
	20	21	22	23	24	25	26	2	3	4	5	6	7	8	Ẓav Shabbat ha-Gadol	
APR	27	28	29	30	31	1	2	9	10	11	12	13	14	**15** Pesaḥ	Pesaḥ	
	3	4	5	6	7	8	9	**16** Pesaḥ	**17** Ḥol ha-Mo'ed	**18** Ḥol ha-Mo'ed	**19** Ḥol ha-Mo'ed	**20** Ḥol ha-Mo'ed	**21** Pesaḥ	**22** Pesaḥ	Pesaḥ	
	10	11	12	13	14	15	16	23	24	25	26	**27** Yom ha-Sho'ah	28	29	Shemini	
	17	18	19	20	21	22	23	**30**	**1**	2	3	4	**5** Yom ha-Aẓma'ut	6	Tazri'a/Meẓora	IYAR
	24	25	26	27	28	29	30	7	8	9	10	11	12	13	Aḥarei Mot/Kedoshim	
MAY	1	2	3	4	5	6	7	14	15	16	17	**18** Lag ba-Omer	19	20	Emor	
	8	9	10	11	12	13	14	21	22	23	24	25	26	27	Be-Har/Be-Ḥukkotai	
	15	16	17	18	19	20	21	**28** Yom Yerushalayim	29	**1**	2	3	4	5	Be-Midbar	SIV
	22	23	24	25	26	27	28	**6** Shavuot	**7** Shavuot	8	9	10	11	12	Naso	
JUNE	29	30	31	1	2	3	4	13	14	15	16	17	18	19	Be-Ha'alotkha	
	5	6	7	8	9	10	11	20	21	22	23	24	25	26	Shelaḥ	
	12	13	14	15	16	17	18	27	28	29	**30**	**1**	2	3	Koraḥ	TAM
	19	20	21	22	23	24	25	4	5	6	7	8	9	10	Ḥukkat	
	26	27	28	29	30			11	12	13	14	15				

988 CIVIL CALENDAR JEWISH CALENDAR 5748/49

	S	M	T	W	T	F	S	S	M	T	W	T	F	S		
JULY						1	2						16	17	Balak	TAM
	3	4	5	6	7	8	9	**18** Fast of Tammuz	19	20	21	22	23	24	Pinḥas	
	10	11	12	13	14	15	16	25	26	27	28	29	**1**	2	Mattot/Masei	AV
	17	18	19	20	21	22	23	3	4	5	6	7	8	9	Devarim Shabbat Ḥazon	
	24	25	26	27	28	29	30	**10** Fast of Av	11	12	13	14	15	16	Va-Ethannan Shabbat Naḥamu	
AUG	31	1	2	3	4	5	6	17	18	19	20	21	22	23	Ekev	
	7	8	9	10	11	12	13	24	25	26	27	28	29	**30**	Re'eh	
	14	15	16	17	18	19	20	**1**	2	3	4	5	6	7	Shofetim	ELUL
	21	22	23	24	25	26	27	8	9	10	11	12	13	14	Ki Teẓe	
SEP	28	29	30	31	1	2	3	15	16	17	18	19	20	21	Ki Tavo	
	4	5	6	7	8	9	10	22	23	24	25	26	27	28	Niẓẓavim	
	11	12	13	14	15	16	17	29	**1** Rosh ha-Shanah	**2** Rosh ha-Shanah	**3** Fast of Gedaliah	4	5	6	Va-Yelekh Shabbat Shuvah	5749
	18	19	20	21	22	23	24	7	8	9	**10** Yom Kippur	11	12	13	Ha'azinu	TISH
OCT	25	26	27	28	29	30	1	14	**15** Sukkot	**16** Sukkot	**17** Hol ha-Mo'ed	**18** Hol ha-Mo'ed	**19** Hol ha-Mo'ed	**20** Hol ha-Mo'ed	Ḥol ha-Mo'ed	
	2	3	4	5	6	7	8	**21** Hoshana Rabba	**22** Shemini Azeret	**23** Simḥat Torah	24	25	26	27	Bereshit	
	9	10	11	12	13	14	15	28	29	**30**	**1**	2	3	4	No'aḥ	ḤESH
	16	17	18	19	20	21	22	5	6	7	8	9	10	11	Lekh Lekha	
	23	24	25	26	27	28	29	12	13	14	15	16	17	18	Va-Yera	
NOV	30	31	1	2	3	4	5	19	20	21	22	23	24	25	Ḥayyei Sarah	
	6	7	8	9	10	11	12	26	27	28	29	**1**	2	3	Toledot	KIS
	13	14	15	16	17	18	19	4	5	6	7	8	9	10	Va-Yeẓe	
	20	21	22	23	24	25	26	11	12	13	14	15	16	17	Va-Yishlaḥ	
DEC	27	28	29	30	1	2	3	18	19	20	21	22	23	24	Va-Yeshev	
	4	5	6	7	8	9	10	**25** Ḥanukkah	**26** Ḥanukkah	**27** Ḥanukkah	**28** Ḥanukkah	**29** Ḥanukkah	**1** Ḥanukkah	**2** Ḥanukkah	Mi-Keẓ	TEV
	11	12	13	14	15	16	17	**3** Ḥanukkah	4	5	6	7	8	9	Va-Yiggash	
	18	19	20	21	22	23	24	**10** Fast of Tevet	11	12	13	14	15	16	Va-Yeḥi	
	25	26	27	28	29	30	31	17	18	19	20	21	22	23	Shemot	

"Oak tree" menorah; silver, parcel gilt; Poland, 19th century. Photograph H.U.C. Skirball Museum.

1989	CIVIL CALENDAR						JEWISH CALENDAR							5749	
	S	M	T	W	T	F	S	S	M	T	W	T	F	S		
JAN	1	2	3	4	5	6	7	24	25	26	27	28	29	**1**	Va-Era	TEV/S
	8	9	10	11	12	13	14	2	3	4	5	6	7	8	Bo	
	15	16	17	18	19	20	21	9	10	11	12	13	14	**15** Tu bi-Shevat	Be-Shallaḥ Shabbat Shirah	
	22	23	24	25	26	27	28	16	17	18	19	20	21	22	Yitro	
FEB	29	30	31	1	2	3	4	23	24	25	26	27	28	29	Mishpatim	
	5	6	7	8	9	10	11	**30**	**1**	2	3	4	5	6	Terumah	
	12	13	14	15	16	17	18	7	8	9	10	11	12	13	Teẓavveh	
	19	20	21	22	23	24	25	14	15	16	17	18	19	20	Ki Tissa	
MAR	26	27	28	1	2	3	4	21	22	23	24	25	26	27	Va-Yakhel Shabbat Shekalim	
	5	6	7	8	9	10	11	28	29	**30**	**1**	2	3	4	Pekudei	ADAR
	12	13	14	15	16	17	18	5	6	7	8	9	10	11	Va-Yikra Shabbat Zakhor	
	19	20	21	22	23	24	25	12	**13** Fast of Esther	**14** Purim	**15** Shushan Purim	16	17	18	Ẓav Shabbat Parah	
APR	26	27	28	29	30	31	1	19	20	21	22	23	24	25	Shemini Shabbat ha-Ḥodesh	
	2	3	4	5	6	7	8	26	27	28	29	**1**	2	3	Tazri'a	NIS
	9	10	11	12	13	14	15	4	5	6	7	8	9	10	Meẓora Shabbat ha-Gadol	
	16	17	18	19	20	21	22	11	12	13	14	**15** Pesaḥ	**16** Pesaḥ	**17** Ḥol ha-Mo'ed	Ḥol ha-Mo'ed	
	23	24	25	26	27	28	29	**18** Ḥol ha-Mo'ed	**19** Ḥol ha-Mo'ed	**20** Ḥol ha-Mo'ed	**21** Pesaḥ	**22** Pesaḥ	23	24	Aḥarei Mot	
MAY	30	1	2	3	4	5	6	25	26	**27** Yom ha-Sho'ah	28	29	**30**	**1**	Kedoshim	IYAR
	7	8	9	10	11	12	13	2	3	4	**5** Yom ha-Aẓma'ut	6	7	8	Emor	
	14	15	16	17	18	19	20	9	10	11	12	13	14	15	Be-Har	
	21	22	23	24	25	26	27	16	17	**18** Lag ba-Omer	**19**	**20**	**21**	**22**	Be-Ḥukkotai	
JUNE	28	29	30	31	1	2	3	23	24	25	26	27	**28** Yom Yerushalayim	29	Be-Midbar	
	4	5	6	7	8	9	10	**1**	2	3	4	5	**6** Shavuot	**7** Shavuot	Shavuot	SIV
	11	12	13	14	15	16	17	8	9	10	11	12	13	14	Naso	
	18	19	20	21	22	23	24	15	16	17	18	19	20	21	Be-Ha'alotkha	
	25	26	27	28	29	30		22	23	24	25	26	27			

	S	M	T	W	T	F	S	S	M	T	W	T	F	S		
JLY							1							28	Shelaḥ	SIV
	2	3	4	5	6	7	8	29	**30**	**1**	2	3	4	5	Koraḥ	TAM
	9	10	11	12	13	14	15	6	7	8	9	10	11	12	Ḥukkat/Balak	
	16	17	18	19	20	21	22	13	14	15	16	**17** Fast of Tammuz	18	19	Pinḥas	
	23	24	25	26	27	28	29	20	21	22	23	24	25	26	Mattot/Masei	
UG	30	31	1	2	3	4	5	27	28	29	**1**	2	3	4	Devarim Shabbat Ḥazon	AV
	6	7	8	9	10	11	12	5	6	7	8	**9** Fast of Av	10	11	Va-Etḥannan Shabbat Naḥamu	
	13	14	15	16	17	18	19	12	13	14	15	16	17	18	Ekev	
	20	21	22	23	24	25	26	19	20	21	22	23	24	25	Re'eh	
EP	27	28	29	30	31	1	2	26	27	28	29	**30**	**1**	2	Shofetim	ELUL
	3	4	5	6	7	8	9	3	4	5	6	7	8	9	Ki Teẓe	
	10	11	12	13	14	15	16	10	11	12	13	14	15	16	Ki Tavo	
	17	18	19	20	21	22	23	17	18	19	20	21	22	23	Niẓẓavim/Va-Yelekh	
	24	25	26	27	28	29	30	24	25	26	27	28	29	**1** Rosh ha-Shanah	Rosh ha-Shanah	5750
CT	1	2	3	4	5	6	7	**2** Rosh ha-Shanah	**3** Fast of Gedaliah	4	5	6	7	8	Ha'azinu Shabbat Shuvah	TISH
	8	9	10	11	12	13	14	9	**10** Yom Kippur	11	12	13	14	**15** Sukkot	Sukkot	
	15	16	17	18	19	20	21	**16** Sukkot	**17** Ḥol ha-Mo'ed	**18** Ḥol ha-Mo'ed	**19** Ḥol ha-Mo'ed	**20** Ḥol ha-Mo'ed	**21** Hoshana Rabba	**22** Shemini Aẓeret	Shemini Aẓeret	
	22	23	24	25	26	27	28	**23** Simḥat Torah	24	25	26	27	28	29	Bereshit	
OV	29	30	31	1	2	3	4	**30**	**1**	2	3	4	5	6	No'aḥ	ḤESH
	5	6	7	8	9	10	11	7	8	9	10	11	12	13	Lekh Lekha	
	12	13	14	15	16	17	18	14	15	16	17	18	19	20	Va-Yera	
	19	20	21	22	23	24	25	21	22	23	24	25	26	27	Ḥayyei Sarah	
EC	26	27	28	29	30	1	2	28	29	**30**	**1**	2	3	4	Toledot	KIS
	3	4	5	6	7	8	9	5	6	7	8	9	10	11	Va-Yeẓe	
	10	11	12	13	14	15	16	12	13	14	15	16	17	18	Va-Yishlaḥ	
	17	18	19	20	21	22	23	19	20	21	22	23	24	**25** Ḥanukkah	Va-Yeshev	
	24	25	26	27	28	29	30	**26** Ḥanukkah	**27** Ḥanukkah	**28** Ḥanukkah	**29** Ḥanukkah	**30** Ḥanukkah	**1** Ḥanukkah	**2** Ḥanukkah	Mi-Keẓ	TEV
	31							3								

כ ת
זאת נדבה
הה פומ כהרר
מאיר בהר רפאל
מהעסונגא
ווזוגתו מרת
לאה בכה זיסל
בינגא מהענא
בשנת תקסול

	S	M	T	W	T	F	S	S	M	T	W	T	F	S		
AN		1	2	3	4	5	6		4	5	6	7	8	9	Va-Yiggash	TEV
	7	8	9	10	11	12	13	**10** Fast of Tevet	11	12	13	14	15	16	Va-Yeḥi	
	14	15	16	17	18	19	20	17	18	19	20	21	22	23	Shemot	
	21	22	23	24	25	26	27	24	25	26	27	28	29	**1**	Va-Era	SHEV
EB	28	29	30	31	1	2	3	2	3	4	5	6	7	8	Bo	
	4	5	6	7	8	9	10	9	10	11	12	13	14	**15** Tu bi-Shevat	Be-Shallaḥ Shabbat Shirah	
	11	12	13	14	15	16	17	16	17	18	19	20	21	22	Yitro	
	18	19	20	21	22	23	24	23	24	25	26	27	28	29	Mishpatim Shabbat Shekalim	
AR	25	26	27	28	1	2	3	**30**	**1**	2	3	4	5	6	Terumah	ADAR
	4	5	6	7	8	9	10	7	8	9	10	**11** Fast of Esther	12	13	Teẓavveh Shabbat Zakhor	
	11	12	13	14	15	16	17	**14** Purim	**15** Shushan Purim	16	17	18	19	20	Ki Tissa Shabbat Parah	
	18	19	20	21	22	23	24	21	22	23	24	25	26	27	Va-Yakhel/Pekudei Shabbat ha-Ḥodesh	
	25	26	27	28	29	30	31	28	29	**1**	2	3	4	5	Va-Yikra	NIS
PR	1	2	3	4	5	6	7	6	7	8	9	10	11	12	Ẓav Shabbat ha-Gadol	
	8	9	10	11	12	13	14	13	14	**15** Pesaḥ	**16** Pesaḥ	**17** Ḥol ha-Mo'ed	**18** Ḥol ha-Mo'ed	**19** Ḥol ha-Mo'ed	Ḥol ha-Mo'ed	
	15	16	17	18	19	20	21	**20** Ḥol ha-Mo'ed	**21** Pesaḥ	**22** Pesaḥ	23	24	25	26	Shemini	
	22	23	24	25	26	27	28	**27** Yom ha-Sho'ah	28	29	**30**	**1**	2	3	Tazri'a/Meẓora	IYAR
AY	29	30	1	2	3	4	5	4	**5** Yom ha-Aẓma'ut	6	7	8	9	10	Aḥarei Mot/ Kedoshim	
	6	7	8	9	10	11	12	11	12	13	14	15	16	17	Emor	
	13	14	15	16	17	18	19	**18** Lag ba-Omer	19	20	21	22	23	24	Be-Har/Be-Ḥukkotai	
	20	21	22	23	24	25	26	25	26	27	**28** Yom Yerushalayim	29	**1**	2	Be-Midbar	SIV
IE	27	28	29	30	31	1	2	3	4	5	**6** Shavuot	**7** Shavuot	8	9	Naso	
	3	4	5	6	7	8	9	10	11	12	13	14	15	16	Be-Ha'alotkha	
	10	11	12	13	14	15	16	17	18	19	20	21	22	23	Shelaḥ	
	17	18	19	20	21	22	23	24	25	26	27	28	29	**30**	Koraḥ	
	24	25	26	27	28	29	30	**1**	2	3	4	5	6	7	Ḥukkat	TAM

ah ark curtain; silk velvet, metallic thread embroidery;
many, 1806. Photograph H.U.C. Skirball Museum.

1990 CIVIL CALENDAR — JEWISH CALENDAR 5750/51

	S	M	T	W	T	F	S	S	M	T	W	T	F	S		
JULY	1	2	3	4	5	6	7	8	9	10	11	12	13	14	Balak	TA
	8	9	10	11	12	13	14	15	16	**17** Fast of Tammuz	18	19	20	21	Pinḥas	
	15	16	17	18	19	20	21	22	23	24	25	26	27	28	Mattot/Masei	
	22	23	24	25	26	27	28	29	**1**	2	3	4	5	6	Devarim Shabbat Ḥazon	AV
AUG	29	30	31	1	2	3	4	7	8	**9** Fast of Av	10	11	12	13	Va-Etḥannan Shabbat Naḥamu	
	5	6	7	8	9	10	11	14	15	16	17	18	19	20	Ekev	
	12	13	14	15	16	17	18	21	22	23	24	25	26	27	Re'eh	
	19	20	21	22	23	24	25	28	29	**30**	**1**	2	3	4	Shofetim	EL
SEP	26	27	28	29	30	31	1	5	6	7	8	9	10	11	Ki Teẓe	
	2	3	4	5	6	7	8	12	13	14	15	16	17	18	Ki Tavo	
	9	10	11	12	13	14	15	19	20	21	22	23	24	25	Niẓẓavim/Va-Yelekh	
	16	17	18	19	20	21	22	26	27	28	29	**1** Rosh ha-Shanah	**2** Rosh ha-Shanah	3	Ha'azinu Shabbat Shuvah	57
	23	24	25	26	27	28	29	**4** Fast of Gedaliah	5	6	7	8	9	**10** Yom Kippur	Yom Kippur	TI
OCT	30	1	2	3	4	5	6	11	12	13	14	**15** Sukkot	**16** Sukkot	**17** Ḥol ha-Mo'ed	Ḥol ha-Mo'ed	
	7	8	9	10	11	12	13	**18** Ḥol ha-Mo'ed	**19** Ḥol ha-Mo'ed	**20** Ḥol ha-Mo'ed	**21** Hoshana Rabba	**22** Shemini Aẓeret	**23** Simḥat Torah	24	Bereshit	
	14	15	16	17	18	19	20	25	26	27	28	29	**30**	**1**	No'aḥ	ḤE
	21	22	23	24	25	26	27	2	3	4	5	6	7	8	Lekh Lekha	
NOV	28	29	30	31	1	2	3	9	10	11	12	13	14	15	Va-Yera	
	4	5	6	7	8	9	10	16	17	18	19	20	21	22	Ḥayyei Sarah	
	11	12	13	14	15	16	17	23	24	25	26	27	28	29	Toledot	
	18	19	20	21	22	23	24	**1**	2	3	4	5	6	7	Va-Yeẓe	KI
DEC	25	26	27	28	29	30	1	8	9	10	11	12	13	14	Va-Yishlaḥ	
	2	3	4	5	6	7	8	15	16	17	18	19	20	21	Va-Yeshev	
	9	10	11	12	13	14	15	22	23	24	**25** Ḥanukkah	**26** Ḥanukkah	**27** Ḥanukkah	**28** Ḥanukkah	Mi-Keẓ	
	16	17	18	19	20	21	22	**29** Ḥanukkah	**30** Ḥanukkah	**1** Ḥanukkah	**2** Ḥanukkah	3	4	5	Va-Yiggash	TE
	23	24	25	26	27	28	29	6	7	8	9	**10** Fast of Tevet	11	12	Va-Yeḥi	
	30	31						13	14							

1991	CIVIL CALENDAR							JEWISH CALENDAR							5751
	S	M	T	W	T	F	S	S	M	T	W	T	F	S		
JAN			1	2	3	4	5			15	16	17	18	19	Shemot	TEV
	6	7	8	9	10	11	12	20	21	22	23	24	25	26	Va-Era	
	13	14	15	16	17	18	19	27	28	29	**1**	2	3	4	Bo	SHEV
	20	21	22	23	24	25	26	5	6	7	8	9	10	11	Be-Shallaḥ Shabbat Shirah	
FEB	27	28	29	30	31	1	2	12	13	14	**15** Tu bi-Shevat	16	17	18	Yitro	
	3	4	5	6	7	8	9	19	20	21	22	23	24	25	Mishpatim Shabbat Shekalim	
	10	11	12	13	14	15	16	26	27	28	29	**30**	**1**	2	Terumah	ADAR
	17	18	19	20	21	22	23	3	4	5	6	7	8	9	Teẓavveh Shabbat Zakhor	
MAR	24	25	26	27	28	1	2	10	11	12	**13** Fast of Esther	**14** Purim	**15** Shushan Purim	16	Ki Tissa	
	3	4	5	6	7	8	9	17	18	19	20	21	22	23	Va-Yakhel/Pekudei Shabbat Parah	
	10	11	12	13	14	15	16	24	25	26	27	28	29	**1**	Va-Yikra Shabbat ha-Ḥodesh	NIS
	17	18	19	20	21	22	23	2	3	4	5	6	7	8	Ẓav Shabbat ha-Gadol	
	24	25	26	27	28	29	30	9	10	11	12	13	14	**15** Pesaḥ	Pesaḥ	
APR	31	1	2	3	4	5	6	**16** Pesaḥ	**17** Ḥol ha-Mo'ed	**18** Ḥol ha-Mo'ed	**19** Ḥol ha-Mo'ed	**20** Ḥol ha-Mo'ed	**21** Pesaḥ	**22**	Pesaḥ	
	7	8	9	10	11	12	13	23	24	25	26	**27** Yom ha-Sho'ah	28	29	Shemini	
	14	15	16	17	18	19	20	**30**	**1**	2	3	4	**5** Yom ha-Aẓma'ut	6	Tazri'a/Meẓora	IYAR
	21	22	23	24	25	26	27	7	8	9	10	11	12	13	Aḥarei Mot/ Kedoshim	
MAY	28	29	30	1	2	3	4	14	15	16	17	**18** Lag ba-Omer	19	20	Emor	
	5	6	7	8	9	10	11	21	22	23	24	25	26	27	Be-Har/Be-Ḥukkotai	
	12	13	14	15	16	17	18	**28** Yom Yerushalayim	29	**1**	2	3	4	5	Be-Midbar	SIV
	19	20	21	22	23	24	25	**6** Shavuot	**7** Shavuot	8	9	10	11	12	Naso	
JUNE	26	27	28	29	30	31	1	13	14	15	16	17	18	19	Be-Ha'alotkha	
	2	3	4	5	6	7	8	20	21	22	23	24	25	26	Shelaḥ	
	9	10	11	12	13	14	15	27	28	29	**30**	**1**	2	3	Koraḥ	TAM
	16	17	18	19	20	21	22	4	5	6	7	8	9	10	Ḥukkat	
	23	24	25	26	27	28	29	11	12	13	14	15	16	17	Balak	
	30							**18** Fast of Tammuz								

1991 CIVIL CALENDAR JEWISH CALENDAR 5751/52

	S	M	T	W	T	F	S	S	M	T	W	T	F	S		
JULY		1	2	3	4	5	6		19	20	21	22	23	24	Pinḥas	TAM
	7	8	9	10	11	12	13	25	26	27	28	29	**1**	2	Mattot/Masei	AV
	14	15	16	17	18	19	20	3	4	5	6	7	8	9	Devarim Shabbat Ḥazon	
	21	22	23	24	25	26	27	**10** Fast of Av	11	12	13	14	15	16	Va-Ethannan Shabbat Naḥamu	
AUG	28	29	30	31	1	2	3	17	18	19	20	21	22	23	Ekev	
	4	5	6	7	8	9	10	24	25	26	27	28	29	**30**	Re'eh	
	11	12	13	14	15	16	17	**1**	2	3	4	5	6	7	Shofetim	ELUL
	18	19	20	21	22	23	24	8	9	10	11	12	13	14	Ki Teẓe	
	25	26	27	28	29	30	31	15	16	17	18	19	20	21	Ki Tavo	
SEP	1	2	3	4	5	6	7	22	23	24	25	26	27	28	Niẓẓavim	
	8	9	10	11	12	13	14	29	**1** Rosh ha-Shanah	**2** Rosh ha-Shanah	**3** Fast of Gedaliah	4	5	6	Va-Yelekh Shabbat Shuvah	5752
	15	16	17	18	19	20	21	7	8	9	**10** Yom Kippur	11	12	13	Ha'azinu	TISH
	22	23	24	25	26	27	28	14	**15** Sukkot	**16** Sukkot	**17** Ḥol ha-Mo'ed	**18** Ḥol ha-Mo'ed	**19** Ḥol ha-Mo'ed	**20** Ḥol ha-Mo'ed	Ḥol ha-Mo'ed	
OCT	29	30	1	2	3	4	5	**21** Hoshana Rabba	**22** Shemini Azeret	**23** Simḥat Torah	24	25	26	27	Bereshit	
	6	7	8	9	10	11	12	28	29	**30**	**1**	2	3	4	No'aḥ	ḤESH
	13	14	15	16	17	18	19	5	6	7	8	9	10	11	Lekh Lekha	
	20	21	22	23	24	25	26	12	13	14	15	16	17	18	Va-Yera	
NOV	27	28	29	30	31	1	2	19	20	21	22	23	24	25	Ḥayyei Sarah	
	3	4	5	6	7	8	9	26	27	28	29	**30**	**1**	2	Toledot	KIS
	10	11	12	13	14	15	16	3	4	5	6	7	8	9	Va-Yeẓe	
	17	18	19	20	21	22	23	10	11	12	13	14	15	16	Va-Yishlaḥ	
	24	25	26	27	28	29	30	17	18	19	20	21	22	23	Va-Yeshev	
DEC	1	2	3	4	5	6	7	24	**25** Ḥanukkah	**26** Ḥanukkah	**27** Ḥanukkah	**28** Ḥanukkah	**29** Ḥanukkah	**30** Ḥanukkah	Mi-Keẓ	
	8	9	10	11	12	13	14	**1** Ḥanukkah	**2** Ḥanukkah	3	4	5	6	7	Va-Yiggash	TEV
	15	16	17	18	19	20	21	8	9	**10** Fast of Tevet	11	12	13	14	Va-Yeḥi	
	22	23	24	25	26	27	28	15	16	17	18	19	20	21	Shemot	
	29	30	31					22	23	24						

he Wandering of Adam and Eve; *lithograph by Abel Pann;*
rusalem, 1920s. Photograph H.U.C. Skirball Museum.

1992 CIVIL CALENDAR — JEWISH CALENDAR 5752

	S	M	T	W	T	F	S	S	M	T	W	T	F	S		
JAN				1	2	3	4				25	26	27	28	Va-Era	TEV
	5	6	7	8	9	10	11	29	**1**	2	3	4	5	6	Bo	SHEV
	12	13	14	15	16	17	18	7	8	9	10	11	12	13	Be-Shallaḥ Shabbat Shirah	
	19	20	21	22	23	24	25	14	**15** Tu bi-Shevat	16	17	18	19	20	Yitro	
FEB	26	27	28	29	30	31	1	21	22	23	24	25	26	27	Mishpatim	
	2	3	4	5	6	7	8	28	29	**30**	**1**	2	3	4	Terumah	ADA
	9	10	11	12	13	14	15	5	6	7	8	9	10	11	Teẓavveh	
	16	17	18	19	20	21	22	12	13	14	15	16	17	18	Ki Tissa	
	23	24	25	26	27	28	29	19	20	21	22	23	24	25	Va-Yakhel Shabbat Shekalim	
MAR	1	2	3	4	5	6	7	26	27	28	29	**30**	**1**	2	Pekudei	ADA
	8	9	10	11	12	13	14	3	4	5	6	7	8	9	Va-Yikra Shabbat Zakhor	
	15	16	17	18	19	20	21	10	11	12	**13** Fast of Esther	**14** Purim	**15** Shushan Purim	16	Ẓav	
	22	23	24	25	26	27	28	17	18	19	20	21	22	23	Shemini Shabbat Parah	
APR	29	30	31	1	2	3	4	24	25	26	27	28	29	**1**	Tazri'a Shabbat ha-Ḥodesh	NIS
	5	6	7	8	9	10	11	2	3	4	5	6	7	8	Meẓora Shabbat ha-Gadol	
	12	13	14	15	16	17	18	9	10	11	12	13	14	**15** Pesaḥ	Pesaḥ	
	19	20	21	22	23	24	25	**16** Pesaḥ	**17** Ḥol ha-Mo'ed	**18** Ḥol ha-Mo'ed	**19** Ḥol ha-Mo'ed	**20** Ḥol ha-Mo'ed	**21** Pesaḥ	**22** Pesaḥ	Pesaḥ	
MAY	26	27	28	29	30	1	2	23	24	25	26	**27** Yom ha-Sho'ah	28	29	Aḥarei Mot	
	3	4	5	6	7	8	9	**30**	**1**	2	3	4	**5** Yom ha-Aẓma'ut	6	Kedoshim	IYA
	10	11	12	13	14	15	16	7	8	9	10	11	12	13	Emor	
	17	18	19	20	21	22	23	14	15	16	17	**18** Lag ba-Omer	19	20	Be-Har	
	24	25	26	27	28	29	30	21	22	23	24	25	26	27	Be-Ḥukkotai	
JUNE	31	1	2	3	4	5	6	**28** Yom Yerushalayim	29	**1**	2	3	4	5	Be-Midbar	SIV
	7	8	9	10	11	12	13	**6** Shavuot	**7** Shavuot	8	9	10	11	12	Naso	
	14	15	16	17	18	19	20	13	14	15	16	17	18	19	Be-Ha'alotkha	
	21	22	23	24	25	26	27	20	21	22	23	24	25	26	Shelaḥ	
	28	29	30					27	28	29						

1992 CIVIL CALENDAR — JEWISH CALENDAR 5752/53

	S	M	T	W	T	F	S	S	M	T	W	T	F	S		
JULY				1	2	3	4				**30**	**1**	2	3	Koraḥ	SIV
	5	6	7	8	9	10	11	4	5	6	7	8	9	10	Ḥukkat	TAM
	12	13	14	15	16	17	18	11	12	13	14	15	16	17	Balak	
	19	20	21	22	23	24	25	**18** Fast of Tammuz	19	20	21	22	23	24	Pinḥas	
AUG	26	27	28	29	30	31	1	25	26	27	28	29	**1**	2	Mattot/Masei	AV
	2	3	4	5	6	7	8	3	4	5	6	7	8	9	Devarim Shabbat Ḥazon	
	9	10	11	12	13	14	15	**10** Fast of Av	11	12	13	14	15	16	Va-Etḥannan Shabbat Naḥamu	
	16	17	18	19	20	21	22	17	18	19	20	21	22	23	Ekev	
	23	24	25	26	27	28	29	24	25	26	27	28	29	**30**	Re'eh	
SEP	30	31	1	2	3	4	5	**1**	2	3	4	5	6	7	Shofetim	ELUL
	6	7	8	9	10	11	12	8	9	10	11	12	13	14	Ki Teẓe	
	13	14	15	16	17	18	19	15	16	17	18	19	20	21	Ki Tavo	
	20	21	22	23	24	25	26	22	23	24	25	26	27	28	Niẓẓavim	
OCT	27	28	29	30	1	2	3	29	**1** Rosh ha-Shanah	**2** Rosh ha-Shanah	**3** Fast of Gedaliah	4	5	6	Va-Yelekh Shabbat Shuvah	5753
	4	5	6	7	8	9	10	7	8	9	**10** Yom Kippur	11	12	13	Ha'azinu	TISH
	11	12	13	14	15	16	17	14	**15** Sukkot	**16** Sukkot	**17** Hol ha-Mo'ed	**18** Hol ha-Mo'ed	**19** Hol ha-Mo'ed	**20** Hol ha-Mo'ed	Ḥol ha-Mo'ed	
	18	19	20	21	22	23	24	**21** Hoshana Rabba	**22** Shemini Azeret	**23** Simḥat Torah	24	25	26	27	Bereshit	
	25	26	27	28	29	30	31	28	29	**30**	**1**	2	3	4	No'aḥ	ḤESH
NOV	1	2	3	4	5	6	7	5	6	7	8	9	10	11	Lekh Lekha	
	8	9	10	11	12	13	14	12	13	14	15	16	17	18	Va-Yera	
	15	16	17	18	19	20	21	19	20	21	22	23	24	25	Ḥayyei Sarah	
	22	23	24	25	26	27	28	26	27	28	29	**1**	2	3	Toledot	KIS
DEC	29	30	1	2	3	4	5	4	5	6	7	8	9	10	Va-Yeẓe	
	6	7	8	9	10	11	12	11	12	13	14	15	16	17	Va-Yishlaḥ	
	13	14	15	16	17	18	19	18	19	20	21	22	23	24	Va-Yeshev	
	20	21	22	23	24	25	26	**25** Ḥanukkah	**26** Ḥanukkah	**27** Ḥanukkah	**28** Ḥanukkah	**29** Ḥanukkah	**1** Ḥanukkah	**2** Ḥanukkah	Mi-Keẓ	TEV
	27	28	29	30	31			**3** Ḥanukkah	4	5	6	7				

993 CIVIL CALENDAR JEWISH CALENDAR 5753

	S	M	T	W	T	F	S	S	M	T	W	T	F	S		
JAN						1	2						8	9	Va-Yiggash	TEV
	3	4	5	6	7	8	9	**10** Fast of Tevet	11	12	13	14	15	16	Va-Yeḥi	
	10	11	12	13	14	15	16	17	18	19	20	21	22	23	Shemot	
	17	18	19	20	21	22	23	24	25	26	27	28	29	**1**	Va-Era	SHEV
	24	25	26	27	28	29	30	2	3	4	5	6	7	8	Bo	
FEB	31	1	2	3	4	5	6	9	10	11	12	13	14	**15** Tu bi-Shevat	Be-Shallaḥ Shabbat Shirah	
	7	8	9	10	11	12	13	16	17	18	19	20	21	22	Yitro	
	14	15	16	17	18	19	20	23	24	25	26	27	28	29	Mishpatim Shabbat Shekalim	
	21	22	23	24	25	26	27	**30**	**1**	2	3	4	5	6	Terumah	ADAR
MAR	28	1	2	3	4	5	6	7	8	9	10	**11** Fast of Esther	12	13	Teẓavveh Shabbat Zakhor	
	7	8	9	10	11	12	13	**14** Purim	**15** Shushan Purim	16	17	18	19	20	Ki Tissa Shabbat Parah	
	14	15	16	17	18	19	20	21	22	23	24	25	26	27	Va-Yakhel/Pekudei Shabbat ha-Ḥodesh	
	21	22	23	24	25	26	27	28	29	**1**	2	3	4	5	Va-Yikra	NIS
APR	28	29	30	31	1	2	3	6	7	8	9	10	11	12	Ẓav Shabbat ha-Gadol	
	4	5	6	7	8	9	10	13	14	**15** Pesaḥ	**16** Pesaḥ	**17** Ḥol ha-Mo’ed	**18** Ḥol ha-Mo’ed	**19** Ḥol ha-Mo’ed	Ḥol ha-Mo’ed	
	11	12	13	14	15	16	17	**20** Ḥol ha-Mo’ed	**21** Pesaḥ	**22** Pesaḥ	23	24	25	26	Shemini	
	18	19	20	21	22	23	24	**27** Yom ha-Sho’ah	28	29	**30**	**1**	2	3	Tazri’a/Meẓora	IYAR
MAY	25	26	27	28	29	30	1	4	**5** Yom ha-Aẓma’ut	6	7	8	9	10	Aḥarei Mot/ Kedoshim	
	2	3	4	5	6	7	8	11	12	13	14	15	16	17	Emor	
	9	10	11	12	13	14	15	**18** Lag ba-Omer	19	20	21	22	23	24	Be-Har/Be-Ḥukkotai	
	16	17	18	19	20	21	22	25	26	27	**28** Yom Yerushalayim	29	**1**	2	Be-Midbar	SIV
	23	24	25	26	27	28	29	3	4	5	**6** Shavuot	**7** Shavuot	8	9	Naso	
UNE	30	31	1	2	3	4	5	10	11	12	13	14	15	16	Be-Ha’alotkha	
	6	7	8	9	10	11	12	17	18	19	20	21	22	23	Shelaḥ	
	13	14	15	16	17	18	19	24	25	26	27	28	29	**30**	Koraḥ	
	20	21	22	23	24	25	26	**1**	2	3	4	5	6	7	Ḥukkat	TAM
	27	28	29	30				8	9	10	11					

rah ark curtain belonging to the Romberg-Glass family;
lk damask, metallic thread embroidery, silk and silk velvet
pliqués; Germany, 1785. Photograph H.U.C. Skirball Museum.

1993	CIVIL CALENDAR							JEWISH CALENDAR								5753/54
	S	M	T	W	T	F	S	S	M	T	W	T	F	S		
JULY					1	2	3					12	13	14	Balak	TAM
	4	5	6	7	8	9	10	15	16	**17** Fast of Tammuz	18	19	20	21	Pinḥas	
	11	12	13	14	15	16	17	22	23	24	25	26	27	28	Mattot/Masei	
	18	19	20	21	22	23	24	29	**1**	2	3	4	5	6	Devarim Shabbat Ḥazon	AV
	25	26	27	28	29	30	31	7	8	**9** Fast of Av	10	11	12	13	Va-Ethannan Shabbat Naḥamu	
AUG	1	2	3	4	5	6	7	14	15	16	17	18	19	20	Ekev	
	8	9	10	11	12	13	14	21	22	23	24	25	26	27	Re'eh	
	15	16	17	18	19	20	21	28	29	**30**	**1**	2	3	4	Shofetim	ELUL
	22	23	24	25	26	27	28	5	6	7	8	9	10	11	Ki Teẓe	
SEP	29	30	31	1	2	3	4	12	13	14	15	16	17	18	Ki Tavo	
	5	6	7	8	9	10	11	19	20	21	22	23	24	25	Niẓẓavim/Va-Yelekh	
	12	13	14	15	16	17	18	26	27	28	29	**1** Rosh ha-Shanah	**2** Rosh ha-Shanah	3	Ha'azinu Shabbat Shuvah	5754
	19	20	21	22	23	24	25	**4** Fast of Gedaliah	5	6	7	8	9	**10** Yom Kippur	Yom Kippur	TISH
OCT	26	27	28	29	30	1	2	11	12	13	14	**15** Sukkot	**16** Sukkot	**17** Ḥol ha-Mo'ed	Ḥol ha-Mo'ed	
	3	4	5	6	7	8	9	**18** Ḥol ha-Mo'ed	**19** Ḥol ha-Mo'ed	**20** Ḥol ha-Mo'ed	**21** Hoshana Rabba	**22** Shemini Aẓeret	**23** Simḥat Torah	24	Bereshit	
	10	11	12	13	14	15	16	25	26	27	28	29	**30**	**1**	No'aḥ	ḤESH
	17	18	19	20	21	22	23	2	3	4	5	6	7	8	Lekh Lekha	
	24	25	26	27	28	29	30	9	10	11	12	13	14	15	Va-Yera	
NOV	31	1	2	3	4	5	6	16	17	18	19	20	21	22	Ḥayyei Sarah	
	7	8	9	10	11	12	13	23	24	25	26	27	28	29	Toledot	
	14	15	16	17	18	19	20	**30**	**1**	2	3	4	5	6	Va-Yeẓe	KIS
	21	22	23	24	25	26	27	7	8	9	10	11	12	13	Va-Yishlaḥ	
DEC	28	29	30	1	2	3	4	14	15	16	17	18	19	20	Va-Yeshev	
	5	6	7	8	9	10	11	21	22	23	24	**25** Ḥanukkah	**26** Ḥanukkah	**27** Ḥanukkah	Mi-Keẓ	
	12	13	14	15	16	17	18	**28** Ḥanukkah	**29** Ḥanukkah	**30** Ḥanukkah	**1** Ḥanukkah	**2** Ḥanukkah	3	4	Va-Yiggash	TEV
	19	20	21	22	23	24	25	5	6	7	8	9	**10** Fast of Tevet	11	Va-Yeḥi	
	26	27	28	29	30	31		12	13	14	15	16	17			

94	CIVIL CALENDAR							JEWISH CALENDAR								5754
	S	M	T	W	T	F	S	S	M	T	W	T	F	S		
JAN							1							18	Shemot	TEV
	2	3	4	5	6	7	8	19	20	21	22	23	24	25	Va-Era	
	9	10	11	12	13	14	15	26	27	28	29	**1**	2	3	Bo	SHEV
	16	17	18	19	20	21	22	4	5	6	7	8	9	10	Be-Shallaḥ Shabbat Shirah	
	23	24	25	26	27	28	29	11	12	13	14	**15** Tu bi-Shevat	16	17	Yitro	
FEB	30	31	1	2	3	4	5	18	19	20	21	22	23	24	Mishpatim	
	6	7	8	9	10	11	12	25	26	27	28	29	**30**	**1**	Terumah Shabbat Shekalim	ADAR
	13	14	15	16	17	18	19	2	3	4	5	6	7	8	Teẓavveh Shabbat Zakhor	
	20	21	22	23	24	25	26	9	10	11	12	**13** Fast of Esther	**14** Purim	**15** Shushan Purim	Ki Tissa	
MAR	27	28	1	2	3	4	5	16	17	18	19	20	21	22	Va-Yakhel Shabbat Parah	
	6	7	8	9	10	11	12	23	24	25	26	27	28	29	Pekudei Shabbat ha-Ḥodesh	
	13	14	15	16	17	18	19	**1**	2	3	4	5	6	7	Va-Yikra	NIS
	20	21	22	23	24	25	26	8	9	10	11	12	13	14	Ẓav Shabbat ha-Gadol	
APR	27	28	29	30	31	1	2	**15** Pesaḥ	**16** Pesaḥ	**17** Ḥol ha-Mo'ed	**18** Ḥol ha-Mo'ed	**19** Ḥol ha-Mo'ed	**20** Ḥol ha-Mo'ed	**21** Pesaḥ	Pesaḥ	
	3	4	5	6	7	8	9	**22** Pesaḥ	23	24	25	26	**27** Yom ha-Sho'ah	28	Shemini	
	10	11	12	13	14	15	16	29	**30**	**1**	2	3	4	**5** Yom ha-Aẓma'ut	Tazri'a/Meẓora	IYAR
	17	18	19	20	21	22	23	6	7	8	9	10	11	12	Aḥarei Mot/ Kedoshim	
	24	25	26	27	28	29	30	13	14	15	16	17	**18** Lag ba-Omer	19	Emor	
MAY	1	2	3	4	5	6	7	20	21	22	23	24	25	26	Be-Har/Be-Ḥukkotai	
	8	9	10	11	12	13	14	27	**28** Yom Yerushalayim	29	**1**	2	3	4	Be-Midbar	SIV
	15	16	17	18	19	20	21	5	**6** Shavuot	**7** Shavuot	8	9	10	11	Naso	
	22	23	24	25	26	27	28	12	13	14	15	16	17	18	Be-Ha'alotkha	
JUNE	29	30	31	1	2	3	4	19	20	21	22	23	24	25	Shelaḥ	
	5	6	7	8	9	10	11	26	27	28	29	**30**	**1**	2	Koraḥ	TAM
	12	13	14	15	16	17	18	3	4	5	6	7	8	9	Ḥukkat	
	19	20	21	22	23	24	25	10	11	12	13	14	15	16	Balak	
	26	27	28	29	30			**17** Fast of Tammuz	18	19	20	21				

994 CIVIL CALENDAR — JEWISH CALENDAR 5754/55

	S	M	T	W	T	F	S	S	M	T	W	T	F	S		
JULY						1	2						22	23	Pinḥas	TAM
	3	4	5	6	7	8	9	24	25	26	27	28	29	**1**	Mattot/Masei	AV
	10	11	12	13	14	15	16	2	3	4	5	6	7	8	Devarim Shabbat Ḥazon	
	17	18	19	20	21	22	23	**9** Fast of Av	10	11	12	13	14	15	Va-Etḥannan Shabbat Naḥamu	
	24	25	26	27	28	29	30	16	17	18	19	20	21	22	Ekev	
AUG	31	1	2	3	4	5	6	23	24	25	26	27	28	29	Re'eh	
	7	8	9	10	11	12	13	**30**	**1**	2	3	4	5	6	Shofetim	ELUL
	14	15	16	17	18	19	20	7	8	9	10	11	12	13	Ki Teẓe	
	21	22	23	24	25	26	27	14	15	16	17	18	19	20	Ki Tavo	
SEP	28	29	30	31	1	2	3	21	22	23	24	25	26	27	Niẓẓavim	
	4	5	6	7	8	9	10	28	29	**1** Rosh ha-Shanah	**2** Rosh ha-Shanah	**3** Fast of Gedaliah	4	5	Va-Yelekh Shabbat Shuvah	5755
	11	12	13	14	15	16	17	6	7	8	9	**10** Yom Kippur	11	12	Ha'azinu	TISH
	18	19	20	21	22	23	24	13	14	**15** Sukkot	**16** Sukkot	**17** Ḥol ha-Mo'ed	**18** Ḥol ha-Mo'ed	**19** Ḥol ha-Mo'ed	Ḥol ha-Mo'ed	
OCT	25	26	27	28	29	30	1	**20** Ḥol ha-Mo'ed	**21** Hoshana Rabba	**22** Shemini Azeret	**23** Simḥat Torah	24	25	26	Bereshit	
	2	3	4	5	6	7	8	27	28	29	**30**	**1**	2	3	No'aḥ	ḤESH
	9	10	11	12	13	14	15	4	5	6	7	8	9	10	Lekh Lekha	
	16	17	18	19	20	21	22	11	12	13	14	15	16	17	Va-Yera	
	23	24	25	26	27	28	29	18	19	20	21	22	23	24	Ḥayyei Sarah	
NOV	30	31	1	2	3	4	5	25	26	27	28	29	**1**	2	Toledot	KIS
	6	7	8	9	10	11	12	3	4	5	6	7	8	9	Va-Yeẓe	
	13	14	15	16	17	18	19	10	11	12	13	14	15	16	Va-Yishlaḥ	
	20	21	22	23	24	25	26	17	18	19	20	21	22	23	Va-Yeshev	
DEC	27	28	29	30	1	2	3	24	**25** Ḥanukkah	**26** Ḥanukkah	**27** Ḥanukkah	**28** Ḥanukkah	**29** Ḥanukkah	**30** Ḥanukkah	Mi-Keẓ	
	4	5	6	7	8	9	10	**1** Ḥanukkah	**2** Ḥanukkah	3	4	5	6	7	Va-Yiggash	TEV
	11	12	13	14	15	16	17	8	9	**10** Fast of Tevet	11	12	13	14	Va-Yeḥi	
	18	19	20	21	22	23	24	15	16	17	18	19	20	21	Shemot	
	25	26	27	28	29	30	31	22	23	24	25	26	27	28	Va-Era	

ynagogue Ḥanukkah menorah; bronze; Aschaffenburg, ermany, 1706. Photograph H.U.C. Skirball Museum.

1995 CIVIL CALENDAR — JEWISH CALENDAR 5755

	S	M	T	W	T	F	S	S	M	T	W	T	F	S		
JAN	1	2	3	4	5	6	7	29	**1**	2	3	4	5	6	Bo	TEV/SH
	8	9	10	11	12	13	14	7	8	9	10	11	12	13	Be-Shallaḥ Shabbat Shirah	
	15	16	17	18	19	20	21	14	**15** Tu bi-Shevat	16	17	18	19	20	Yitro	
	22	23	24	25	26	27	28	21	22	23	24	25	26	27	Mishpatim	
FEB	29	30	31	1	2	3	4	28	29	**30**	**1**	2	3	4	Terumah	ADAR I
	5	6	7	8	9	10	11	5	6	7	8	9	10	11	Teẓavveh	
	12	13	14	15	16	17	18	12	13	14	15	16	17	18	Ki Tissa	
	19	20	21	22	23	24	25	19	20	21	22	23	24	25	Va Yakhel Shabbat Shekalim	
MAR	26	27	28	1	2	3	4	26	27	28	29	**30**	**1**	2	Pekudei	ADAR II
	5	6	7	8	9	10	11	3	4	5	6	7	8	9	Va-Yikra Shabbat Zakhor	
	12	13	14	15	16	17	18	10	11	12	**13** Fast of Esther	**14** Purim	**15** Shushan Purim	16	Ẓav	
	19	20	21	22	23	24	25	17	18	19	20	21	22	23	Shemini Shabbat Parah	
APR	26	27	28	29	30	31	1	24	25	26	27	28	29	**1**	Tazri'a Shabbat ha-Ḥodesh	NIS
	2	3	4	5	6	7	8	2	3	4	5	6	7	8	Meẓora Shabbat ha-Gadol	
	9	10	11	12	13	14	15	9	10	11	12	13	14	**15** Pesaḥ	Pesaḥ	
	16	17	18	19	20	21	22	**16** Pesaḥ	**17** Ḥol ha-Mo'ed	**18** Ḥol ha-Mo'ed	**19** Ḥol ha-Mo'ed	**20** Ḥol ha-Mo'ed	**21** Pesaḥ	**22** Pesaḥ	Pesaḥ	
	23	24	25	26	27	28	29	23	24	25	26	**27** Yom ha-Sho'ah	28	29	Aḥarei Mot	
MAY	30	1	2	3	4	5	6	**30**	**1**	2	3	4	**5** Yom ha-Aẓma'ut	6	Kedoshim	IYAR
	7	8	9	10	11	12	13	7	8	9	10	11	12	13	Emor	
	14	15	16	17	18	19	20	14	15	16	17	**18** Lag ba-Omer	19	20	Be-Har	
	21	22	23	24	25	26	27	21	22	23	24	25	26	27	Be-Ḥukkotai	
JUNE	28	29	30	31	1	2	3	**28** Yom Yerushalayim	29	**1**	2	3	4	5	Be-Midbar	SIV
	4	5	6	7	8	9	10	**6** Shavuot	**7** Shavuot	8	9	10	11	12	Naso	
	11	12	13	14	15	16	17	13	14	15	16	17	18	19	Be-Ha'alotkha	
	18	19	20	21	22	23	24	20	21	22	23	24	25	26	Shelaḥ	
	25	26	27	28	29	30		27	28	29	**30**	**1**	2			TAM

	S	M	T	W	T	F	S	S	M	T	W	T	F	S		
JULY							1							3	Koraḥ	TAM
	2	3	4	5	6	7	8	4	5	6	7	8	9	10	Ḥukkat	
	9	10	11	12	13	14	15	11	12	13	14	15	16	17	Balak	
	16	17	18	19	20	21	22	**18** Fast of Tammuz	19	20	21	22	23	24	Pinḥas	
	23	24	25	26	27	28	29	25	26	27	28	29	**1**	2	Mattot/Masei	AV
AUG	30	31	1	2	3	4	5	3	4	5	6	7	8	9	Devarim Shabbat Ḥazon	
	6	7	8	9	10	11	12	**10** Fast of Av	11	12	13	14	15	16	Va-Ethannan Shabbat Naḥamu	
	13	14	15	16	17	18	19	17	18	19	20	21	22	23	Ekev	
	20	21	22	23	24	25	26	24	25	26	27	28	29	**30**	Re'eh	
SEP	27	28	29	30	31	1	2	**1**	2	3	4	5	6	7	Shofetim	ELUL
	3	4	5	6	7	8	9	8	9	10	11	12	13	14	Ki Teẓe	
	10	11	12	13	14	15	16	15	16	17	18	19	20	21	Ki Tavo	
	17	18	19	20	21	22	23	22	23	24	25	26	27	28	Niẓẓavim	
	24	25	26	27	28	29	30	29	**1** Rosh ha-Shanah	**2** Rosh ha-Shanah	**3** Fast of Gedaliah	4	5	6	Va-Yelekh Shabbat Shuvah	5756
OCT	1	2	3	4	5	6	7	7	8	9	**10** Yom Kippur	11	12	13	Ha'azinu	TISH
	8	9	10	11	12	13	14	14	**15** Sukkot	**16** Sukkot	**17** Ḥol ha-Mo'ed	**18** Ḥol ha-Mo'ed	**19** Ḥol ha-Mo'ed	**20** Ḥol ha-Mo'ed	Ḥol ha-Mo'ed	
	15	16	17	18	19	20	21	**21** Hoshana Rabba	**22** Shemini Azeret	**23** Simḥat Torah	24	25	26	27	Bereshit	
	22	23	24	25	26	27	28	28	29	**30**	**1**	2	3	4	Noaḥ	ḤESH
NOV	29	30	31	1	2	3	4	5	6	7	8	9	10	11	Lekh Lekha	
	5	6	7	8	9	10	11	12	13	14	15	16	17	18	Va-Yera	
	12	13	14	15	16	17	18	19	20	21	22	23	24	25	Ḥayyei Sarah	
	19	20	21	22	23	24	25	26	27	28	29	**30**	**1**	2	Toledot	KIS
DEC	26	27	28	29	30	1	2	3	4	5	6	7	8	9	Va-Yeẓe	
	3	4	5	6	7	8	9	10	11	12	13	14	15	16	Va-Yishlaḥ	
	10	11	12	13	14	15	16	17	18	19	20	21	22	23	Va-Yeshev	
	17	18	19	20	21	22	23	24	**25** Ḥanukkah	**26** Ḥanukkah	**27** Ḥanukkah	**28** Ḥanukkah	**29** Ḥanukkah	**30** Ḥanukkah	Mi-Keẓ	
	24	25	26	27	28	29	30	**1** Ḥanukkah	**2** Ḥanukkah	3	4	5	6	7	Va-Yiggash	TEV
	31							8								

	S	M	T	W	T	F	S		S	M	T	W	T	F	S		
JAN		1	2	3	4	5	6	....		9	**10** Fast of Tevet	11	12	13	14	Va-Yeḥi	TEV
	7	8	9	10	11	12	13	....	15	16	17	18	19	20	21	Shemot	
	14	15	16	17	18	19	20	....	22	23	24	25	26	27	28	Va-Era	SHEV
	21	22	23	24	25	26	27	....	29	**1**	2	3	4	5	6	Bo	
FEB	28	29	30	31	1	2	3	....	7	8	9	10	11	12	13	Be-Shallaḥ Shabbat Shirah	
	4	5	6	7	8	9	10	....	14	**15** Tu bi-Shevat	16	17	18	19	20	Yitro	
	11	12	13	14	15	16	17	....	21	22	23	24	25	26	27	Mishpatim Shabbat Shekalim	
	18	19	20	21	22	23	24	....	28	29	**30**	**1**	2	3	4	Terumah	ADAR
AR	25	26	27	28	29	1	2	....	5	6	7	8	9	10	11	Teẓavveh Shabbat Zakhor	
	3	4	5	6	7	8	9	....	12	**13** Fast of Esther	**14** Purim	**15** Shushan Purim	16	17	18	Ki Tissa Shabbat Parah	
	10	11	12	13	14	15	16	....	19	20	21	22	23	24	25	Va-Yakhel/Pekudei Shabbat ha-Ḥodesh	
	17	18	19	20	21	22	23	....	26	27	28	29	**1**	2	3	Va-Yikra	NIS
	24	25	26	27	28	29	30	....	4	5	6	7	8	9	10	Ẓav Shabbat ha-Gadol	
PR	31	1	2	3	4	5	6	....	11	12	13	14	**15** Pesaḥ	**16** Pesaḥ	**17** Ḥol ha-Mo'ed	Ḥol ha-Mo'ed	
	7	8	9	10	11	12	13	....	**18** Ḥol ha-Mo'ed	**19** Ḥol ha-Mo'ed	**20** Ḥol ha-Mo'ed	**21** Pesaḥ	**22** Pesaḥ	23	24	Shemini	
	14	15	16	17	18	19	20	....	25	26	**27** Yom ha-Sho'ah	28	29	**30**	**1**	Tazri'a/Meẓora	IYAR
	21	22	23	24	25	26	27	....	2	3	4	**5** Yom ha-Aẓma'ut	6	7	8	Aḥarei Mot/ Kedoshim	
AY	28	29	30	1	2	3	4	....	9	10	11	12	13	14	15	Emor	
	5	6	7	8	9	10	11	....	16	17	**18** Lag ba-Omer	19	20	21	22	Be-Har/Be-Ḥukkotai	
	12	13	14	15	16	17	18	....	23	24	25	26	27	**28** Yom Yerushalayim	29	Be-Midbar	
	19	20	21	22	23	24	25	....	**1**	2	3	4	5	**6** Shavuot	**7** Shavuot	Shavuot	SIV
NE	26	27	28	29	30	31	1	....	8	9	10	11	12	13	14	Naso	
	2	3	4	5	6	7	8	....	15	16	17	18	19	20	21	Be-Ha'alotkha	
	9	10	11	12	13	14	15	....	22	23	24	25	26	27	28	Shelaḥ	TAM
	16	17	18	19	20	21	22	....	29	**30**	**1**	2	3	4	5	Koraḥ	
	23	24	25	26	27	28	29	....	6	7	8	9	10	11	12	Ḥukkat/Balak	
	30							....	13								

Sabbath lamp; silver, by Valentin Schuler; Frankfurt, Germany, late 17th century. Photograph H.U.C. Skirball Museum.

1996 CIVIL CALENDAR JEWISH CALENDAR 5756/57

	S	M	T	W	T	F	S	S	M	T	W	T	F	S		
JULY		1	2	3	4	5	6		14	15	16	**17** Fast of Tammuz	18	19	Pinḥas	TA
	7	8	9	10	11	12	13	20	21	22	23	24	25	26	Mattot/Masei	
	14	15	16	17	18	19	20	27	28	29	**1**	2	3	4	Devarim Shabbat Ḥazon	AV
	21	22	23	24	25	26	27	5	6	7	8	**9** Fast of Av	10	11	Va-Ethannan Shabbat Naḥamu	
AUG	28	29	30	31	1	2	3	12	13	14	15	16	17	18	Ekev	
	4	5	6	7	8	9	10	19	20	21	22	23	24	25	Re'eh	
	11	12	13	14	15	16	17	26	27	28	29	**30**	**1**	2	Shofetim	EL
	18	19	20	21	22	23	24	3	4	5	6	7	8	9	Ki Teẓe	
	25	26	27	28	29	30	31	10	11	12	13	14	15	16	Ki Tavo	
SEP	1	2	3	4	5	6	7	17	18	19	20	21	22	23	Niẓẓavim/Va-Yelekh	
	8	9	10	11	12	13	14	24	25	26	27	28	29	**1** Rosh ha-Shanah	Rosh ha-Shanah	57
	15	16	17	18	19	20	21	**2** Rosh ha-Shanah	**3** Fast of Gedaliah	4	5	6	7	8	Ha'azinu Shabbat Shuvah	TI
	22	23	24	25	26	27	28	9	**10** Yom Kippur	11	12	13	14	**15** Sukkot	Sukkot	
OCT	29	30	1	2	3	4	5	**16** Sukkot	**17** Ḥol ha-Mo'ed	**18** Ḥol ha-Mo'ed	**19** Ḥol ha-Mo'ed	**20** Ḥol ha-Mo'ed	**21** Hoshana Rabba	**22** Shemini Aẓeret	Shemini Aẓeret	
	6	7	8	9	10	11	12	**23** Simḥat Torah	24	25	26	27	28	29	Bereshit	
	13	14	15	16	17	18	19	**30**	**1**	2	3	4	5	6	Noaḥ	Ḥ
	20	21	22	23	24	25	26	7	8	9	10	11	12	13	Lekh Lekha	
NOV	27	28	29	30	31	1	2	14	15	16	17	18	19	20	Va-Yera	
	3	4	5	6	7	8	9	21	22	23	24	25	26	27	Ḥayyei Sarah	
	10	11	12	13	14	15	16	28	29	**1**	2	3	4	5	Toledot	K
	17	18	19	20	21	22	23	6	7	8	9	10	11	12	Va-Yeẓe	
	24	25	26	27	28	29	30	13	14	15	16	17	18	19	Va-Yishlaḥ	
DEC	1	2	3	4	5	6	7	20	21	22	23	24	**25** Ḥanukkah	**26** Ḥanukkah	Va-Yeshev	
	8	9	10	11	12	13	14	**27** Ḥanukkah	**28** Ḥanukkah	**29** Ḥanukkah	**1** Ḥanukkah	**2** Ḥanukkah	**3** Ḥanukkah	4	Mi-Keẓ	T
	15	16	17	18	19	20	21	5	6	7	8	9	**10** Fast of Tevet	11	Va-Yiggash	
	22	23	24	25	26	27	28	12	13	14	15	16	17	18	Va-Yeḥi	
	29	30	31					19	20	21						

997 CIVIL CALENDAR — JEWISH CALENDAR 5757

	S	M	T	W	T	F	S	S	M	T	W	T	F	S		
JAN				1	2	3	4				22	23	24	25	Shemot	TEV
	5	6	7	8	9	10	11	26	27	28	29	**1**	2	3	Va-Era	SHEV
	12	13	14	15	16	17	18	4	5	6	7	8	9	10	Bo	
	19	20	21	22	23	24	25	11	12	13	14	**15** Tu bi-Shevat	16	17	Be-Shallaḥ Shabbat Shirah	
FEB	26	27	28	29	30	31	1	18	19	20	21	22	23	24	Yitro	
	2	3	4	5	6	7	8	25	26	27	28	29	**30**	**1**	Mishpatim	ADAR I
	9	10	11	12	13	14	15	2	3	4	5	6	7	8	Terumah	
	16	17	18	19	20	21	22	9	10	11	12	13	14	15	Teẓavveh	
MAR	23	24	25	26	27	28	1	16	17	18	19	20	21	22	Ki Tissa	
	2	3	4	5	6	7	8	23	24	25	26	27	28	29	Va-Yakhel Shabbat Shekalim	
	9	10	11	12	13	14	15	**30**	**1**	2	3	4	5	6	Pekudei	ADAR II
	16	17	18	19	20	21	22	7	8	9	10	**11** Fast of Esther	12	13	Va-Yikra Shabbat Zakhor	
	23	24	25	26	27	28	29	**14** Purim	**15** Shushan Purim	16	17	18	19	20	Ẓav Shabbat Parah	
APR	30	31	1	2	3	4	5	21	22	23	24	25	26	27	Shemini Shabbat ha-Ḥodesh	
	6	7	8	9	10	11	12	28	29	**1**	2	3	4	5	Tazri'a	NIS
	13	14	15	16	17	18	19	6	7	8	9	10	11	12	Meẓora Shabbat ha-Gadol	
	20	21	22	23	24	25	26	13	14	**15** Pesaḥ	**16** Pesaḥ	**17** Ḥol ha-Mo'ed	**18** Ḥol ha-Mo'ed	**19** Ḥol ha-Mo'ed	Ḥol ha-Mo'ed	
MAY	27	28	29	30	1	2	3	**20** Ḥol ha-Mo'ed	**21** Pesaḥ	**22** Pesaḥ	23	24	25	26	Aḥarei Mot	
	4	5	6	7	8	9	10	**27** Yom ha-Sho'ah	28	29	**30**	**1**	2	3	Kedoshim	IYAR
	11	12	13	14	15	16	17	4	**5** Yom ha-Aẓma'ut	6	7	8	9	10	Emor	
	18	19	20	21	22	23	24	11	12	13	14	15	16	17	Be-Har	
	25	26	27	28	29	30	31	**18** Lag ba-Omer	19	20	21	22	23	24	Be-Ḥukkotai	
JUNE	1	2	3	4	5	6	7	25	26	27	**28** Yom Yerushalayim	29	**1**	2	Be-Midbar	SIV
	8	9	10	11	12	13	14	3	4	5	**6** Shavuot	**7** Shavuot	8	9	Naso	
	15	16	17	18	19	20	21	10	11	12	13	14	15	16	Be-Ha'alotkha	
	22	23	24	25	26	27	28	17	18	19	20	21	22	23	Shelaḥ	
	29	30						24	25							

ושמרו בני ישראל
את השבת
השירים אשר לשלמה
שמעון
לוי
יהודה
בנימין
יששכר
יוסף
נפתלי
אשר
גד
דן

997 CIVIL CALENDAR — JEWISH CALENDAR 5757/58

	S	M	T	W	T	F	S	S	M	T	W	T	F	S		
JULY			1	2	3	4	5			26	27	28	29	**30**	Koraḥ	SIV
	6	7	8	9	10	11	12	**1**	2	3	4	5	6	7	Ḥukkat	TAM
	13	14	15	16	17	18	19	8	9	10	11	12	13	14	Balak	
	20	21	22	23	24	25	26	15	16	**17** Fast of Tammuz	18	19	20	21	Pinḥas	
AUG	27	28	29	30	31	1	2	22	23	24	25	26	27	28	Mattot/Masei	
	3	4	5	6	7	8	9	29	**1**	2	3	4	5	6	Devarim Shabbat Ḥazon	AV
	10	11	12	13	14	15	16	7	8	**9** Fast of Av	10	11	12	13	Va-Etḥannan Shabbat Naḥamu	
	17	18	19	20	21	22	23	14	15	16	17	18	19	20	Ekev	
	24	25	26	27	28	29	30	21	22	23	24	25	26	27	Re'eh	
SEP	31	1	2	3	4	5	6	28	29	**30**	**1**	2	3	4	Shofetim	ELUL
	7	8	9	10	11	12	13	5	6	7	8	9	10	11	Ki Teẓe	
	14	15	16	17	18	19	20	12	13	14	15	16	17	18	Ki Tavo	
	21	22	23	24	25	26	27	19	20	21	22	23	24	25	Niẓẓavim/Va-Yelekh	
OCT	28	29	30	1	2	3	4	26	27	28	29	**1** Rosh ha-Shanah	**2** Rosh ha-Shanah	3	Ha'azinu Shabbat Shuvah	5758
	5	6	7	8	9	10	11	**4** Fast of Gedaliah	5	6	7	8	9	**10** Yom Kippur	Yom Kippur	TISH
	12	13	14	15	16	17	18	11	12	13	14	**15** Sukkot	**16** Sukkot	**17** Ḥol ha-Mo'ed	Ḥol ha-Mo'ed	
	19	20	21	22	23	24	25	**18** Ḥol ha-Mo'ed	**19** Ḥol ha-Mo'ed	**20** Ḥol ha-Mo'ed	**21** Hoshana Rabba	**22** Shemini Aẓeret	**23** Simḥat Torah	24	Bereshit	
NOV	26	27	28	29	30	31	1	25	26	27	28	29	**30**	**1**	Noaḥ	ḤESH
	2	3	4	5	6	7	8	2	3	4	5	6	7	8	Lekh Lekha	
	9	10	11	12	13	14	15	9	10	11	12	13	14	15	Va-Yera	
	16	17	18	19	20	21	22	16	17	18	19	20	21	22	Ḥayyei Sarah	
	23	24	25	26	27	28	29	23	24	25	26	27	28	29	Toledot	
DEC	30	1	2	3	4	5	6	**1**	2	3	4	5	6	7	Va-Yeẓe	KIS
	7	8	9	10	11	12	13	8	9	10	11	12	13	14	Va-Yishlaḥ	
	14	15	16	17	18	19	20	15	16	17	18	19	20	21	Va-Yeshev	
	21	22	23	24	25	26	27	22	23	24	**25** Ḥanukkah	**26** Ḥanukkah	**27** Ḥanukkah	**28** Ḥanukkah	Mi-Keẓ	
	28	29	30	31				**29** Ḥanukkah	**30** Ḥanukkah	**1** Ḥanukkah	**2** Ḥanukkah					TEV

llah cover; silk batik, braid trim; early
th century. Photograph H.U.C. Skirball Museum.

1998 CIVIL CALENDAR — JEWISH CALENDAR 5758

	S	M	T	W	T	F	S	S	M	T	W	T	F	S		
JAN					1	2	3					3	4	5	Va-Yiggash	TEV
	4	5	6	7	8	9	10	6	7	8	9	**10** Fast of Tevet	11	12	Va-Yeḥi	
	11	12	13	14	15	16	17	13	14	15	16	17	18	19	Shemot	
	18	19	20	21	22	23	24	20	21	22	23	24	25	26	Va-Era	
	25	26	27	28	29	30	31	27	28	29	**1**	2	3	4	Bo	SHEV
FEB	1	2	3	4	5	6	7	5	6	7	8	9	10	11	Be-Shallaḥ Shabbat Shirah	
	8	9	10	11	12	13	14	12	13	14	**15** Tu bi-Shevat	16	17	18	Yitro	
	15	16	17	18	19	20	21	19	20	21	22	23	24	25	Mishpatim Shabbat Shekalim	
	22	23	24	25	26	27	28	26	27	28	29	**30**	**1**	2	Terumah	ADA
MAR	1	2	3	4	5	6	7	3	4	5	6	7	8	9	Tezavveh Shabbat Zakhor	
	8	9	10	11	12	13	14	10	11	12	**13** Fast of Esther	**14** Purim	**15** Shushan Purim	16	Ki-Tissa	
	15	16	17	18	19	20	21	17	18	19	20	21	22	23	Va-Yakhel/Pekudei Shabbat Parah	
	22	23	24	25	26	27	28	24	25	26	27	28	29	**1**	Va-Yikra Shabbat ha-Ḥodesh	NIS
APR	29	30	31	1	2	3	4	2	3	4	5	6	7	8	Ẓav Shabbat ha-Gadol	
	5	6	7	8	9	10	11	9	10	11	12	13	14	**15** Pesaḥ	Pesaḥ	
	12	13	14	15	16	17	18	**16** Pesaḥ	**17** Ḥol ha-Mo'ed	**18** Ḥol ha-Mo'ed	**19** Ḥol ha-Mo'ed	**20** Ḥol ha-Mo'ed	**21** Pesaḥ	**22** Pesaḥ	Pesaḥ	
	19	20	21	22	23	24	25	23	24	25	26	**27** Yom ha-Sho'ah	28	29	Shemini	
MAY	26	27	28	29	30	1	2	**30**	**1**	2	3	4	**5** Yom ha-Aẓma'ut	6	Tazri'a/Meẓora	IYA
	3	4	5	6	7	8	9	7	8	9	10	11	12	13	Aḥarei Mot/ Kedoshim	
	10	11	12	13	14	15	16	14	15	16	17	**18** Lag ba-Omer	19	20	Emor	
	17	18	19	20	21	22	23	21	22	23	24	25	26	27	Be-Har/Be-Ḥukkotai	
	24	25	26	27	28	29	30	**28** Yom Yerushalayim	29	**1**	2	3	4	5	Be-Midbar	SIV
JUNE	31	1	2	3	4	5	6	**6** Shavuot	**7** Shavuot	8	9	10	11	12	Naso	
	7	8	9	10	11	12	13	13	14	15	16	17	18	19	Be-Ha'alotkha	
	14	15	16	17	18	19	20	20	21	22	23	24	25	26	Shelaḥ	
	21	22	23	24	25	26	27	27	28	29	**30**	**1**	2	3	Koraḥ	TA
	28	29	30					4	5	6						

998 CIVIL CALENDAR JEWISH CALENDAR 5758/59

	S	M	T	W	T	F	S	S	M	T	W	T	F	S		
JULY				1	2	3	4				7	8	9	10	Ḥukkat	TAM
	5	6	7	8	9	10	11	11	12	13	14	15	16	17	Balak	
	12	13	14	15	16	17	18	**18** Fast of Tammuz	19	20	21	22	23	24	Pinḥas	
	19	20	21	22	23	24	25	25	26	27	28	29	**1**	2	Mattot/Masei	AV
AUG	26	27	28	29	30	31	1	3	4	5	6	7	8	9	Devarim Shabbat Ḥazon	
	2	3	4	5	6	7	8	**10** Fast of Av	11	12	13	14	15	16	Va-Etḥannan Shabbat Naḥamu	
	9	10	11	12	13	14	15	17	18	19	20	21	22	23	Ekev	
	16	17	18	19	20	21	22	24	25	26	27	28	29	**30**	Re'eh	
	23	24	25	26	27	28	29	**1**	2	3	4	5	6	7	Shofetim	ELUL
SEP	30	31	1	2	3	4	5	8	9	10	11	12	13	14	Ki Teẓe	
	6	7	8	9	10	11	12	15	16	17	18	19	20	21	Ki Tavo	
	13	14	15	16	17	18	19	22	23	24	25	26	27	28	Niẓẓavim	
	20	21	22	23	24	25	26	29	**1** Rosh ha-Shanah	**2** Rosh ha-Shanah	**3** Fast of Gedaliah	4	5	6	Va-Yelekh Shabbat Shuvah	5759
OCT	27	28	29	30	1	2	3	7	8	9	**10** Yom Kippur	11	12	13	Ha'azinu	TISH
	4	5	6	7	8	9	10	14	**15** Sukkot	**16** Sukkot	**17** Ḥol ha-Mo'ed	**18** Ḥol ha-Mo'ed	**19** Ḥol ha-Mo'ed	**20** Ḥol ha-Mo'ed	Ḥol ha-Mo'ed	
	11	12	13	14	15	16	17	**21** Hoshana Rabba	**22** Shemini Aẓeret	**23** Simḥat Torah	24	25	26	27	Bereshit	
	18	19	20	21	22	23	24	28	29	**30**	**1**	2	3	4	No'aḥ	ḤESH
	25	26	27	28	29	30	31	5	6	7	8	9	10	11	Lekh Lekha	
NOV	1	2	3	4	5	6	7	12	13	14	15	16	17	18	Va-Yera	
	8	9	10	11	12	13	14	19	20	21	22	23	24	25	Ḥayyei Sarah	
	15	16	17	18	19	20	21	26	27	28	29	**30**	**1**	2	Toledot	KIS
	22	23	24	25	26	27	28	3	4	5	6	7	8	9	Va-Yeẓe	
DEC	29	30	1	2	3	4	5	10	11	12	13	14	15	16	Va-Yishlaḥ	
	6	7	8	9	10	11	12	17	18	19	20	21	22	23	Va-Yeshev	
	13	14	15	16	17	18	19	24	**25** Ḥanukkah	**26** Ḥanukkah	**27** Ḥanukkah	**28** Ḥanukkah	**29** Ḥanukkah	**30** Ḥanukkah	Mi-Keẓ	
	20	21	22	23	24	25	26	**1** Ḥanukkah	**2** Ḥanukkah	3	4	5	6	7	Va-Yiggash	TEV
	27	28	29	30	31			8	9	**10** Fast of Tevet	11	12				

בסימנא טבא ובמזלא מעליא
בששי

1999 CIVIL CALENDAR — JEWISH CALENDAR 5759

	S	M	T	W	T	F	S	S	M	T	W	T	F	S		
JAN						1	2						13	14	Va-Yeḥi	TEV
	3	4	5	6	7	8	9	15	16	17	18	19	20	21	Shemot	
	10	11	12	13	14	15	16	22	23	24	25	26	27	28	Va-Era	
	17	18	19	20	21	22	23	29	**1**	2	3	4	5	6	Bo	SHEV
	24	25	26	27	28	29	30	7	8	9	10	11	12	13	Be-Shallaḥ Shabbat Shirah	
FEB	31	1	2	3	4	5	6	14	**15** Tu bi-Shevat	16	17	18	19	20	Yitro	
	7	8	9	10	11	12	13	21	22	23	24	25	26	27	Mishpatim Shabbat Shekalim	
	14	15	16	17	18	19	20	28	29	**30**	**1**	2	3	4	Terumah	ADAR
	21	22	23	24	25	26	27	5	6	7	8	9	10	11	Tezavveh Shabbat Zakhor	
MAR	28	1	2	3	4	5	6	12	**13** Fast of Esther	**14** Purim	**15** Shushan Purim	16	17	18	Ki Tissa Shabbat Parah	
	7	8	9	10	11	12	13	19	20	21	22	23	24	25	Va-Yakhel/Pekudei Shabbat ha-Ḥodesh	
	14	15	16	17	18	19	20	26	27	28	29	**1**	2	3	Va-Yikra	NIS
	21	22	23	24	25	26	27	4	5	6	7	8	9	10	Zav Shabbat ha-Gadol	
APR	28	29	30	31	1	2	3	11	12	13	14	**15** Pesaḥ	**16** Pesaḥ	**17** Ḥol ha-Mo'ed	Ḥol ha-Mo'ed	
	4	5	6	7	8	9	10	**18** Ḥol ha-Mo'ed	**19** Ḥol ha-Mo'ed	**20** Ḥol ha-Mo'ed	**21** Pesaḥ	**22** Pesaḥ	23	24	Shemini	
	11	12	13	14	15	16	17	25	26	**27** Yom ha-Sho'ah	28	29	**30**	**1**	Tazri'a/Mezora	IYAR
	18	19	20	21	22	23	24	2	3	4	**5** Yom ha-Azma'ut	6	7	8	Aḥarei Mot/ Kedoshim	
MAY	25	26	27	28	29	30	1	9	10	11	12	13	14	15	Emor	
	2	3	4	5	6	7	8	16	17	**18** Lag ba-Omer	19	20	21	22	Be-Har/Be-Ḥukkotai	
	9	10	11	12	13	14	15	23	24	25	26	27	**28** Yom Yerushalayim	29	Be-Midbar	
	16	17	18	19	20	21	22	**1**	2	3	4	5	**6** Shavuot	**7** Shavuot	Shavuot	SIV
	23	24	25	26	27	28	29	8	9	10	11	12	13	14	Naso	
JUNE	30	31	1	2	3	4	5	15	16	17	18	19	20	21	Be-Ha'alotkha	
	6	7	8	9	10	11	12	22	23	24	25	26	27	28	Shelaḥ	
	13	14	15	16	17	18	19	29	**30**	**1**	2	3	4	5	Koraḥ	TAM
	20	21	22	23	24	25	26	6	7	8	9	10	11	12	Ḥukkat/Balak	
	27	28	29	30				13	14	15	16					

Ketubbah; parchment, tempera and ink; Spilimbergo, Italy, 1752. Photograph H.U.C. Skirball Museum.

1999 CIVIL CALENDAR — JEWISH CALENDAR 5759/60

	S	M	T	W	T	F	S	S	M	T	W	T	F	S		
JULY					1	2	3					**17** Fast of Tammuz	18	19	Pinḥas	TAM
	4	5	6	7	8	9	10	20	21	22	23	24	25	26	Mattot/Masei	
	11	12	13	14	15	16	17	27	28	29	**1**	2	3	4	Devarim Shabbat Ḥazon	AV
	18	19	20	21	22	23	24	5	6	7	8	**9** Fast of Av	10	11	Va-Ethannan Shabbat Naḥamu	
	25	26	27	28	29	30	31	12	13	14	15	16	17	18	Ekev	
AUG	1	2	3	4	5	6	7	19	20	21	22	23	24	25	Re'eh	
	8	9	10	11	12	13	14	26	27	28	29	**30**	**1**	2	Shofetim	ELUL
	15	16	17	18	19	20	21	3	4	5	6	7	8	9	Ki Teẓe	
	22	23	24	25	26	27	28	10	11	12	13	14	15	16	Ki Tavo	
SEP	29	30	31	1	2	3	4	17	18	19	20	21	22	23	Niẓẓavim/Va-Yelekh	
	5	6	7	8	9	10	11	24	25	26	27	28	29	**1** Rosh ha-Shanah	Rosh ha-Shanah	5760
	12	13	14	15	16	17	18	**2** Rosh ha-Shanah	**3** Fast of Gedaliah	4	5	6	7	8	Ha'azinu Shabbat Shuvah	TISH
	19	20	21	22	23	24	25	9	**10** Yom Kippur	11	12	13	14	**15** Sukkot	Sukkot	
OCT	26	27	28	29	30	1	2	**16** Sukkot	**17** Ḥol ha-Mo'ed	**18** Ḥol ha-Mo'ed	**19** Ḥol ha-Mo'ed	**20** Ḥol ha-Mo'ed	**21** Hoshana Rabba	**22** Shemini Aẓeret	Shemini Aẓeret	
	3	4	5	6	7	8	9	**23** Simḥat Torah	24	25	26	27	28	29	Bereshit	
	10	11	12	13	14	15	16	**30**	**1**	2	3	4	5	6	No'aḥ	ḤESH
	17	18	19	20	21	22	23	7	8	9	10	11	12	13	Lekh Lekha	
	24	25	26	27	28	29	30	14	15	16	17	18	19	20	Va-Yera	
NOV	31	1	2	3	4	5	6	21	22	23	24	25	26	27	Ḥayyei Sarah	
	7	8	9	10	11	12	13	28	29	**30**	**1**	2	3	4	Toledot	KIS
	14	15	16	17	18	19	20	5	6	7	8	9	10	11	Va-Yeẓe	
	21	22	23	24	25	26	27	12	13	14	15	16	17	18	Va-Yishlaḥ	
DEC	28	29	30	1	2	3	4	19	20	21	22	23	24	**25** Ḥanukkah	Va-Yeshev	
	5	6	7	8	9	10	11	**26** Ḥanukkah	**27** Ḥanukkah	**28** Ḥanukkah	**29** Ḥanukkah	**30** Ḥanukkah	**1** Ḥanukkah	**2** Ḥanukkah	Mi-Keẓ	TEV
	12	13	14	15	16	17	18	3	4	5	6	7	8	9	Va-Yiggash	
	19	20	21	22	23	24	25	**10** Fast of Tevet	11	12	13	14	15	16	Va-Yeḥi	
	26	27	28	29	30	31		17	18	19	20	21	22			

000 CIVIL CALENDAR — JEWISH CALENDAR 5760

	S	M	T	W	T	F	S	S	M	T	W	T	F	S		
JAN							1							23	Shemot	TEV
	2	3	4	5	6	7	8	24	25	26	27	28	29	**1**	Va-Era	SHEV
	9	10	11	12	13	14	15	2	3	4	5	6	7	8	Bo	
	16	17	18	19	20	21	22	9	10	11	12	13	14	**15** Tu bi-Shevat	Be-Shallaḥ Shabbat Shirah	
	23	24	25	26	27	28	29	16	17	18	19	20	21	22	Yitro	
FEB	30	31	1	2	3	4	5	23	24	25	26	27	28	29	Mishpatim	
	6	7	8	9	10	11	12	**30**	**1**	2	3	4	5	6	Terumah	ADAR I
	13	14	15	16	17	18	19	7	8	9	10	11	12	13	Teẓavveh	
	20	21	22	23	24	25	26	14	15	16	17	18	19	20	Ki Tissa	
MAR	27	28	29	1	2	3	4	21	22	23	24	25	26	27	Va-Yakhel Shabbat Shekalim	
	5	6	7	8	9	10	11	28	29	**30**	**1**	2	3	4	Pekudei	ADAR II
	12	13	14	15	16	17	18	5	6	7	8	9	10	11	Va-Yikra Shabbat Zakhor	
	19	20	21	22	23	24	25	12	**13** Fast of Esther	**14** Purim	**15** Shushan Purim	16	17	18	Ẓav Shabbat Parah	
APR	26	27	28	29	30	31	1	19	20	21	22	23	24	25	Shemini Shabbat ha-Ḥodesh	
	2	3	4	5	6	7	8	26	27	28	29	**1**	2	3	Tazri'a	NIS
	9	10	11	12	13	14	15	4	5	6	7	8	9	10	Meẓora Shabbat ha-Gadol	
	16	17	18	19	20	21	22	11	12	13	14	**15** Pesaḥ	**16** Pesaḥ	**17** Ḥol ha-Mo'ed	Ḥol ha-Mo'ed	
	23	24	25	26	27	28	29	**18** Ḥol ha-Mo'ed	**19** Ḥol ha-Mo'ed	**20** Ḥol ha-Mo'ed	**21** Pesaḥ	**22** Pesaḥ	23	24	Aḥarei Mot	
MAY	30	1	2	3	4	5	6	25	26	**27** Yom ha-Sho'ah	28	29	**30**	**1**	Kedoshim	IYAR
	7	8	9	10	11	12	13	2	3	4	**5** Yom ha-Aẓma'ut	6	7	8	Emor	
	14	15	16	17	18	19	20	9	10	11	12	13	14	15	Be-Har	
	21	22	23	24	25	26	27	16	17	**18** Lag ba-Omer	19	20	21	22	Be-Ḥukkotai	
JUNE	28	29	30	31	1	2	3	23	24	25	26	27	**28** Yom Yerushalayim	29	Be-Midbar	
	4	5	6	7	8	9	10	**1**	2	3	4	5	**6** Shavuot	**7** Shavuot	Shavuot	SIV
	11	12	13	14	15	16	17	8	9	10	11	12	13	14	Naso	
	18	19	20	21	22	23	24	15	16	17	18	19	20	21	Be-Ha'alotkha	
	25	26	27	28	29	30		22	23	24	25	26	27			

2000 CIVIL CALENDAR — JEWISH CALENDAR 5760

	S	M	T	W	T	F	S	S	M	T	W	T	F	S		
JULY							1							28	Shelaḥ	SIV
	2	3	4	5	6	7	8	29	**30**	**1**	2	3	4	5	Koraḥ	TAM
	9	10	11	12	13	14	15	6	7	8	9	10	11	12	Ḥukkat/Balak	
	16	17	18	19	20	21	22	13	14	15	16	**17** Fast of Tammuz	18	19	Pinḥas	
	23	24	25	26	27	28	29	20	21	22	23	24	25	26	Mattot/Masei	
AUG	30	31	1	2	3	4	5	27	28	29	**1** Fast of Av	2	3	4	Devarim Shabbat Ḥazon	AV
	6	7	8	9	10	11	12	5	6	7	8	**9**	10	11	Va-Ethannan Shabbat Naḥamu	
	13	14	15	16	17	18	19	12	13	14	15	16	17	18	Ekev	
	20	21	22	23	24	25	26	19	20	21	22	23	24	25	Re'eh	
SEP	27	28	29	30	31	1	2	26	27	28	29	**30**	**1**	2	Shofetim	ELUL
	3	4	5	6	7	8	9	3	4	5	6	7	8	9	Ki Teẓe	
	10	11	12	13	14	15	16	10	11	12	13	14	15	16	Ki Tavo	
	17	18	19	20	21	22	23	17	18	19	20	21	22	23	Niẓẓavim/Va-Yelekh	
	24	25	26	27	28	29	30	24	25	26	27	28	29	**1** Rosh ha-Shanah	Rosh ha-Shanah	5761
OCT	1	2	3	4	5	6	7	**2** Rosh ha-Shanah	**3** Fast of Gedaliah	4	5	6	7	8	Ha'azinu Shabbat Shuvah	TISH
	8	9	10	11	12	13	14	9	**10** Yom Kippur	11	12	13	14	**15** Sukkot	Sukkot	
	15	16	17	18	19	20	21	**16** Sukkot	**17** Ḥol ha-Mo'ed	**18** Ḥol ha-Mo'ed	**19** Ḥol ha-Mo'ed	**20** Ḥol ha-Mo'ed	**21** Hoshana Rabba	**22** Shemini Aẓeret	Shemini Aẓeret	
	22	23	24	25	26	27	28	**23** Simḥat Torah	24	25	26	27	28	29	Bereshit	
NOV	29	30	31	1	2	3	4	**30**	**1**	2	3	4	5	6	No'aḥ	HESH
	5	6	7	8	9	10	11	7	8	9	10	11	12	13	Lekh Lekha	
	12	13	14	15	16	17	18	14	15	16	17	18	19	20	Va-Yera	
	19	20	21	22	23	24	25	21	22	23	24	25	26	27	Ḥayyei Sarah	
DEC	26	27	28	29	30	1	2	28	29	**1**	2	3	4	5	Toledot	KIS
	3	4	5	6	7	8	9	6	7	8	9	10	11	12	Va-Yeẓe	
	10	11	12	13	14	15	16	13	14	15	16	17	18	19	Va-Yishlaḥ	
	17	18	19	20	21	22	23	20	21	22	23	24	**25** Ḥanukkah	**26** Ḥanukkah	Va-Yeshev	
	24	25	26	27	28	29	30	**27** Ḥanukkah	**28** Ḥanukkah	**29** Ḥanukkah	**1** Ḥanukkah	**2** Ḥanukkah	**3** Ḥanukkah	4	Mi-Keẓ	TEV
	31							5								

THE YAHRZEIT

Each year, on the anniversary of the death of a relative or a friend, it is customary to light a memorial candle. The candle is lit on the evening before and is allowed to burn through the day of the Yahrzeit (literally: "year's time"). If the Yahrzeit coincides with the Sabbath or a Yom Tov, the Yahrzeit candle is lit prior to lighting the Sabbath or Yom Tov candles.

A memorial prayer, *El Malei Raḥamim*, is generally recited in the synagogue on the Sabbath preceding the Yahrzeit. The Mourner's Kaddish is recited in the presence of a minyan on the day of the Yahrzeit. One who is observing a Yahrzeit generally conducts all the services, beginning with the evening service of the preceding day. If one does not know how to lead the service, one should still attend the services in order to recite the Mourner's Kaddish. It is customary to visit the grave of the deceased on the day of the Yahrzeit. At the cemetery one should recite psalms and *El Malei Raḥamim*. One should also make a charitable donation in memory of the deceased. Another traditional practice is to study a portion from the Mishnah (in either Hebrew or English). If that is not possible, one should study a chapter of the Bible (again, in either Hebrew or English).

YAHRZEIT RECORDS

English Name

Hebrew Name

Relationship

Date of birth | Date of death | Jewish calendar date of death

English Name

Hebrew Name

Relationship

Date of birth | Date of death | Jewish calendar date of death

English Name

Hebrew Name

Relationship

Date of birth | Date of death | Jewish calendar date of death

YAHRZEIT RECORDS

English Name

Hebrew Name

Relationship

Date of birth | Date of death | Jewish calendar date of death

English Name

Hebrew Name

Relationship

Date of birth | Date of death | Jewish calendar date of death

English Name

Hebrew Name

Relationship

Date of birth | Date of death | Jewish calendar date of death

MOURNER'S KADDISH

Magnified and sanctified be His Great Name in the world which He hath created according to His will. May He establish His Kingdom during your life and during your days, and during the life of the whole household of Israel, even speedily and in a near time! So say ye "Amen."

Let His Great Name be blessed forever and unto all eternity!

Blessed, praised, and glorified, exalted, extolled, and honored, uplifted and lauded, be the name of the Holy One, blessed be He! above all the blessings and hymns, the praises and consolations, which are uttered in the world. So say ye "Amen."

May there be abundant peace from Heaven and life for us and all Israel! So say ye "Amen."

He who maketh peace in His Heights, may He make peace for us and all Israel! So say ye "Amen."

MOURNER'S KADDISH

Yis-gadal ve-yis-kadash she-may rabbo be-olmo deeve-ro chiroosay. Ve-yamlich malchoosay be-cha-yay-chown u-ve-yomaychown, u-ve-cha-yay de-chol bais yisro'ayl, ba-agolo u-vis-man koreev. Ve-imroo omayn.

Ye-hay she-may rabbo me-vorach le-olam u-le-olmay olma-yoh.

Yis-borach, ve-yish-tabach, ve-yis-po'ar, ve-yis-romam, ve-yis-nasay, ve-yis-hadar, ve-yis-alleh, ve-yis-hallol, she-may de-koodsho, be-rich hoo, le-eylo min kol birchoso ve-sheeroso, toosh-bechoso ve-ne-che-moso, da-ameeron be-olmo. Ve-im-roo omayn.

Ye-hay she-lomo rabbo min she-mayo ve-chayim olaynoo ve-al kol yisro'ayl. Ve-imroo omayn.

Oseh sholom bimromov, hoo ya-aseh sholom olaynoo ve-al kol yisro'ayl. Ve-imroo omayn.

קַדִּישׁ יָתוֹם

יִתְגַּדַּל וְיִתְקַדַּשׁ שְׁמֵהּ רַבָּא בְּעָלְמָא דִּי בְרָא כִרְעוּתֵהּ. וְיַמְלִיךְ מַלְכוּתֵהּ בְּחַיֵּיכוֹן וּבְיוֹמֵיכוֹן, וּבְחַיֵּי דְכָל־בֵּית יִשְׂרָאֵל, בַּעֲגָלָא וּבִזְמַן קָרִיב. וְאִמְרוּ אָמֵן.

יְהֵא שְׁמֵהּ רַבָּא מְבָרַךְ לְעָלַם וּלְעָלְמֵי עָלְמַיָּא.

יִתְבָּרַךְ, וְיִשְׁתַּבַּח, וְיִתְפָּאַר, וְיִתְרוֹמַם, וְיִתְנַשֵּׂא, וְיִתְהַדַּר, וְיִתְעַלֶּה וְיִתְהַלַּל שְׁמֵהּ דְּקֻדְשָׁא בְּרִיךְ הוּא, לְעֵלָּא (לְעֵלָּא) מִן כָּל־בִּרְכָתָא וְשִׁירָתָא, תֻּשְׁבְּחָתָא וְנֶחֱמָתָא, דַּאֲמִירָן בְּעָלְמָא. וְאִמְרוּ אָמֵן.

יְהֵא שְׁלָמָא רַבָּא מִן שְׁמַיָּא וְחַיִּים עָלֵינוּ וְעַל כָּל־יִשְׂרָאֵל. וְאִמְרוּ אָמֵן.

עוֹשֶׂה שָׁלוֹם בִּמְרוֹמָיו, הוּא יַעֲשֶׂה שָׁלוֹם עָלֵינוּ וְעַל כָּל־יִשְׂרָאֵל. וְאִמְרוּ אָמֵן.